William T. Poague as Captain

Gunner with Stonewall

Reminiscences of
WILLIAM THOMAS POAGUE

*Lieutenant, Captain, Major and Lieutenant Colonel of
Artillery, Army of Northern Virginia, CSA, 1861-65*

A MEMOIR WRITTEN FOR HIS CHILDREN IN 1903

Edited by
MONROE F. COCKRELL

With an Introduction by
BELL IRVIN WILEY

INTRODUCTION TO THE BISON BOOKS EDITION
BY ROBERT K. KRICK

University of Nebraska Press
Lincoln and London

Introduction to the Bison Books Edition © 1998 by the University of Nebraska
Press
Manufactured in the United States of America

♾

First Bison Books printing: 1998
Most recent printing indicated by the last digit below:
10   9   8   7   6   5   4   3   2   1

Library of Congress Cataloging-in-Publication Data
Poague, William Thomas, 1835–1914.
Gunner with Stonewall: reminiscences of William Thomas Poague, lieutenant,
captain, major, and lieutenant colonel of artillery, Army of Northern Virginia,
CSA, 1861–65: a memoir written for his children in 1903 / edited by Monroe
F. Cockrell; with an introduction by Bell Irvin Wiley.
p.   cm.
Originally published: Jackson, Tenn.: McCowat-Mercer Press, 1957.
Includes bibliographical references (p.   ) and index.
ISBN 0-8032-8753-4 (pbk.: alk. paper)
1. Poague, William Thomas, 1835–1914.   2. Jackson, Stonewall, 1824–
1863—Friends and associates.   3. United States—History—Civil War, 1861–
1865—Personal narratives, Confederate.   4. Confederate States of America.
Army of Northern Virginia—History.   5. United States—History—Civil War,
1861–1865—Regimental histories.   6. Soldiers—Southern States—Biography.
I. Cockrell, Monroe F. (Monroe Fulkerson), b. 1884.   II. Title.
E605.P6   1998
973.7'455—dc21
98-8000   CIP

Reprinted from the original 1957 edition by McCowat-Mercer Press, Inc.,
Jackson TN.

INTRODUCTION TO THE BISON BOOKS EDITION

Robert K. Krick

The *San Francisco Chronicle* called William T. Poague's *Gunner with Stonewall* "one of the best of the recent crop of Civil War literature" when the book appeared in 1957. Many other crops have been harvested in that genre during the four decades since, but Poague's memoir remains "one of the best." The book's considerable intrinsic merits and the author's decidedly unusual perspective are certain to keep it in that distinguished category.

Memoirs by members of R. E. Lee's famous Army of Northern Virginia always have attracted a wide audience. Some such books deservedly have become classics; a gratifyingly large sample include fascinating and useful material, at least intermittently; those of another, lower tier hardly deserved publication but sell nonetheless because of the insatiable public appetite for an inside look at the army and its soldiery.

Among the amazing flood of soldier narratives, artillerists remain notably underrepresented. Chronicles of the experiences of infantrymen abound. Books by cavalrymen who fought in Virginia have appeared in print in numbers disproportionate to their participation, even beyond the level of their musket-toting comrades in infantry units. For some reason the men of Lee's "Long Arm" have consumed less ink, relative to their numbers and the importance of their role, than their comrades of the other arms. The standard Civil War military bibliography (published in 1967), for instance, shows not a single separately printed memoir by an artillerist in Lee's army from Alabama, Georgia, Mississippi, or North Carolina.

The relatively short roster of artillerist memoirs from the Army of Northern Virginia does include some that must be accorded status as admirable standard sources: William Miller Owen on the Washington Artillery of New Orleans; R. Snowden Andrews of Maryland; a small but splendid history of South Carolina's Pee Dee Artillery; and classic books by Virginian gunners (most of them noncommissioned ranks) Carlton McCarthy, William Meade Dame, Robert Stiles, Joseph A. Graves, C. A. Fonerden, Frederick S. Daniel, George M. Neese, Francis W. Dawson, R. C. M. Page, Royal W. Figg, John J. Shoemaker, and Edward A. Moore. The 1989 publication of the memoirs of General Edward Porter Alexander (*Fighting for the Confederacy*, University of North Carolina Press, ed. Gary W.

Gallagher) stands as the best single Confederate artillery book extant, a distinction it is likely to retain permanently.

What Poague affords that none of the others do, their considerable merits notwithstanding, is the perspective of an artillery battalion commander during the main campaigns in the eastern theater. The switch to a battalion system in the winter of 1862-63 was one of the most significant wartime adjustments effected within the Army of Northern Virginia. It constituted an empirical reaction to the exigencies of the first modern war. Poague's promotion to a majority, and his assignment as executive officer of one of the new battalions, coincided with the reorganization. He had been a lieutenant for twelve months and a captain and battery commander for eleven months. Poague's rank as major lasted for eleven more months, and then from February 1864 until Appomattox he commanded his own battalion as a lieutenant colonel.

Five others among the good artillery memoirs are by men who held field-grade rank, but none of them commanded a battalion—that innovative tactical formation—with the main army for an extended period. Owen served for a long spell away from the primary theater as a major and only achieved battalion-commander rank six weeks before Appomattox. Andrews suffered a ghastly wound the summer before the battalion system was implemented and had only been back on duty for a few weeks before another wound took him out of the war. Stiles never advanced beyond the rank of major, and that quite late and with responsibilities for fixed batteries rather than field artillery. Page also never advanced beyond major and was assigned primarily to southwestern Virginia; his book in any case is concerned almost entirely with his original battery. The matchless Alexander, by contrast, was promoted beyond battalion rank in midwar and even before that had been utilized in acting and de facto roles of higher responsibility.

Battalion commander Poague stands alone in the catalog of Confederate memoirists as a chronicler at that level for the campaigns of the Army of Northern Virginia in 1864. Furthermore, Poague's credentials as a narrator put him in a class by himself in a far larger category. Remarkably, there exists no major published memoir by a field-grade officer of any arm, not just artillery, for the army's Third Corps. No other battalion or brigade commander among that rather broad cross-section of the army has appeared extensively in print. Charles Richardson, D. G. McIntosh, James H. Lane, Nathaniel H. Harris, and William Mahone all wrote in passing, but nothing of book length. That leaves Poague's book not only the best but essentially the *only* primary memoir about the Third Corps from the perspective of a ranking officer.

Poague's first North American ancestor, Robert Poage (the adjustment to

Poague came later), had settled three miles north of Staunton, Virginia, by 1738. The first documented European establishment in the vicinity dates from only a dozen years earlier. By the time of the Civil War, the clan had not spread more than a few-score miles away from that initial Poage settlement.

Robert came to Virginia from Ireland, where all of his children but the last had been born. His son Thomas, born in Virginia in 1739, married Mary McClanahan, daughter of an Irishman who had become sheriff of Augusta County. Their son John, born in 1771, married the widowed Mrs. Rachel Barclay Crawford, who begat John Barclay Poague in 1805. The first child of J. B. Poague and his bride, Elizabeth Stuart Paxton, was a boy destined to become the Gunner with Stonewall. (This paragraph, in sketchily tracing Colonel Poague's roots, enumerates between middle names and surnames a goodly proportion of the most prominent families of Augusta and Rockbridge Counties at the time of the Civil War.)

William Thomas Poague was born five days before the Christmas of 1835, in Rockbridge County. His life and career would be firmly rooted in that sylvan corner of Virginia's lovely valley. William worked on his father's farm as a youngster and attended the old field schools of the neighborhood. In 1857 Poague received an A.B. degree from Washington College. (For twenty years beginning in 1865 he would serve as a trustee of his alma mater, including General Lee's entire tenure as president of the school that soon would also bear his name.) Young Poague taught school for a year near Atlanta in the late 1850s, then returned to Lexington to study law. Admitted to the Missouri bar, William practiced for a time in St. Joseph during 1860. By year's end he had returned to Lexington and entered into a legal partnership. Poague's anti-secessionist Whig political leanings hardly qualified him as one of Lexington's rebels in the making.

Nothing in that background, solid though it was, suggested preparation for a prominent role amid the biggest war in American annals. A combination of energy, aptitude, and good fortune, however, catapulted Poague through four promotions, eventually planting him near the top of the artillery hierarchy of the Army of Northern Virginia. The Rockbridge Artillery, which Poague joined as an enlisted man before winning prompt election as lieutenant, was among the half-dozen most famous Confederate batteries. That distinction was earned on many a battlefield but burnished notably by association with the famous Stonewall Brigade and its eponymous commander. On April 22, 1862, Poague became captain of the renowned battery. His commission as major dated from March 2, 1863, and he became a lieutenant colonel on February 27, 1864.

The 1863 promotion resulted in large part from a personal recommendation by Lee. Almost every family of Confederate descendants can report lore about kind words from the legendary Lee concerning their ancestors, but few of those tales can be traced in primary documents. Poague's can. His 1864 promotion was buttressed by an endorsement from General William Nelson Pendleton—the army's chief of artillery and a fellow Lexingtonian. The general was widely, and accurately, considered an unredeemed disaster in the field (albeit administratively steady), so his support was of uncertain utility. On January 24, 1865, Pendleton warmly recommended Poague for promotion to full colonel, but that commission was not issued during the few weeks of life left to the Confederacy. Poague surrendered at Appomattox as a lieutenant colonel, claiming one horse as his private property.

The ex-Confederate made as thorough a success of his postwar life as he had of his military career. He abandoned the legal profession, taught school briefly, became a successful Rockbridge farmer, won a seat in the Virginia legislature, and then for thirty years served as treasurer of Virginia Military Institute (VMI). Poague discharged his duties in that responsible role with the same calm, modest demeanor that had won him battlefield promotions. When a general assembly committee applauded him for the institute's bookkeeping system, Poague simply said that the system was not of his devising but rather came from "a skilful accountant." Any changes in the future he would select upon the advice of "an expert accountant—one who is practical and sensible in his views, after a full acquaintance with the conditions here." That well-modulated management style and personality prompted an institute observer to say of Poague, "His very presence was a benediction." Another applauded the colonel's "high purpose . . . honest mind . . . strong common sense . . . great industry, patience and care . . . faithfulness and efficiency." General George Catlett Marshall, who graduated from VMI in 1901, wrote of the colonel: "He was a very silent little man and it never dawned on me that he was a great warrior in his youth."

Poague avoided domestic entanglements until six days past his forty-third birthday, when he married Josephine Moore. The couple had four children (all three sons graduated from VMI). He maintained unswerving devotion to the same Presbyterian Church, indeed the same congregation, that had been the bulwark of his pious commander early in the war, Thomas J. "Stonewall" Jackson.

The old colonel retained a strong affinity for his wartime comrades, not long before his death riding in a parade at the head of the original guns with which the Rockbridge Artillery had gone to war. Late in life he wrote extensively for the historical columns of the *Richmond Times-Dispatch*. When a veteran of Poague's battery sought a pension in Texas, the sometime captain obligingly mailed a signed deposition to support the application.

Correspondence with officer veterans and with prospective authors survives to tell us much about Poague's experiences and views. The aging colonel responded to a query from fellow Virginian John Warwick Daniel "with pleasure" and assured Daniel that anything he wrote would be "of great interest to . . . us old Confederates who may be spared to see it." When Captain Fred Colston, working on an article about artillery service, solicited a photograph, Poague sent a likeness in captain's uniform. "I have also one as Maj of Arty which makes me somewhat better looking," the colonel added drolly, "but I would rather be known as the Captain of the Rock[bridge] Arty. than any other position with which I was honored." Josephine Poague agreed about the relative merits of the photos—in fact she probably was the source of the judgment in the first place—and on her prompting the colonel sent the second photo to Colston with a postscript. Unfortunately, the photo at higher rank seems not to have survived, so we can only imagine the handsome version of Colonel Poague.

When he died on September 8, 1914, Poague was buried a few feet from the grave of his old commander, Stonewall Jackson.

Poague's written legacy, *Gunner with Stonewall*, benefited from no known diary and was written several decades after the events it described. The memoir is far more interesting and important than it otherwise would be because of its originally intended audience. Since he was writing for his children and other family members, not for publication, Poague felt no obligation to honor late-Victorian strictures against identifying individuals and passing subjective judgments. For instance, despite his undisguised admiration for Lee, Poague described the arrival of one of the general's sons as seeming "as if an iceberg had floated into the room." The pretentious Lee son exuded "such frigid dignity" that Poague and John Pelham—himself far more famous than this icy Lee—were "completely frozen out." Another Lee son, who served in Poague's battery, appears in a warm, amusing story about a surprise encounter with his famous father. Then again the memoirist describes army commander Lee chewing out gunner Poague.

Those portions of *Gunner with Stonewall* that can be checked against other sources most always prove to be accurate, with only occasional errors on minor points. Poague's informed, uninhibited remarks about superior officers are deliciously quotable, but his sketches of his peers and subordinate enlisted men often are even better. The most important material in the book is about Poague's experiences in the artillery position at Prospect Hill during the Battle of Fredericksburg and in the Widow Tapp's

Field at the time of the famous Lee-to-the-Rear episode in the Wilderness. Poague reported that those suffering at the former location renamed the height "Dead Horse Hill," a designation that has gained wide usage. His description of the episode in which the Texas Brigade turned Lee back in the Wilderness is among the very best of the primary accounts of that dramatic affair. Other chapters treat military events in Virginia with an appealing mixture of verve and pathos.

These attributes prompted Hal Bridges, writing for the *American Historical Review*, to describe *Gunner with Stonewall* as "lively and useful." *Civil War History*, then the leading scholarly journal on the period, called Poague's narrative "lucid . . . colorful, honest, perceptive." The memoir is all of that, which has won it a niche on most historians' shelves of Best Books About Lee's Army.

BIBLIOGRAPHIC NOTE

The following sources include information about Poague's life, career, and memoirs: Robert Bell Woodworth, comp., *The Descendants of Robert and John Poage* (Staunton VA, 1954); Poague's official Compiled Service Record in Roll 199, M331, National Archives; *In Memoriam, William Thomas Poague* (Lexington VA, 1914); Poague file, Virginia Military Institute Archives; reviews of *Gunner with Stonewall* in *San Francisco Chronicle* (July 28, 1957), *Chicago Sunday Tribune* (November 17, 1957), *Civil War History* (December 1957), and *American Historical Review* (January 1958); Poague to F. M. Colston, July 5, 1911, Campbell Family Papers, Southern Historical Collection, University of North Carolina; Robert K. Krick, "'Lee to the Rear,' The Texans Cried," in Gary W. Gallagher, ed., *The Wilderness Campaign* (Chapel Hill NC, 1997); Edward A. Moore, "Col. William T. Poague," *Confederate Veteran*, November 1914; Jennings Cropper Wise, *The Long Arm of Lee*, 2 vols. (Lynchburg VA, 1915); *Richmond Times-Dispatch*, September 24, 1905, and August 20 and 27, 1914; expanded Virginia volume, *Confederate Military History* (Atlanta GA, 1899); July 1862 Poague report in Box 31, Civil War Miscellaneous Collection, Yale University; Poague letters of March 29, 1904 (regarding Wilderness), and August 8, 1905 (regarding 1st Manassas), in Boxes 23 and 22, John Warwick Daniel Papers, University of Virginia; and Jennings Cropper Wise, "Poague in the Wilderness," *The Cadet*, vol. 7, no. 1 (September 16, 1914).

TABLE OF CONTENTS

ILLUSTRATIONS

The Military Campaigns of Stonewall Jackson

PREPARED BY MONROE F. COCKRELL

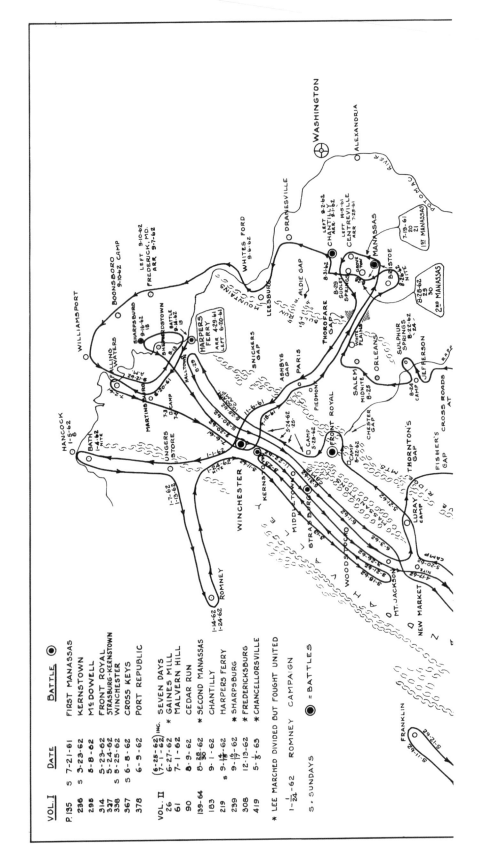

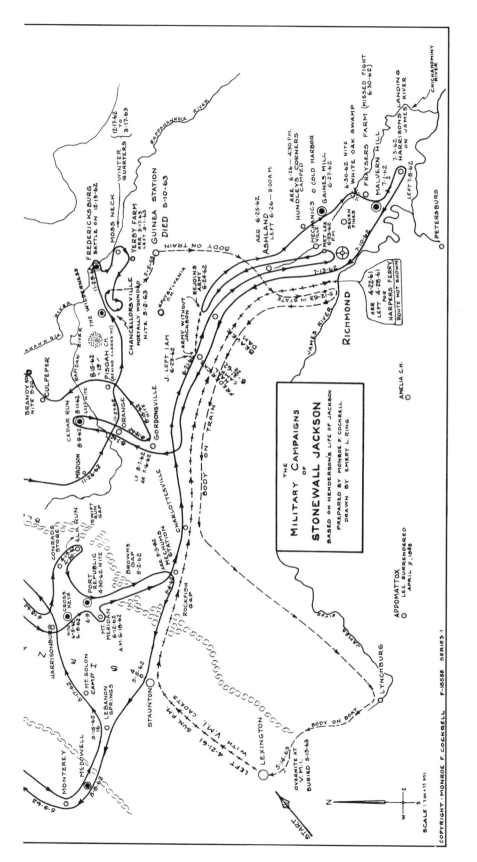

THE
MILITARY CAMPAIGNS
OF
STONEWALL JACKSON
BASED ON HENDERSON'S LIFE OF JACKSON
PREPARED BY MONROE F. COCKRELL
DRAWN BY EMERY L. RING

SCALE: 1 IN = 11 MI.

COPYRIGHT - MONROE F. COCKRELL   F-18556   SERIES 1

EDITOR'S FOREWORD

In the summer of 1951 while sitting out under the trees with classmates at VMI, I first heard of these reminiscences. Naturally I was aroused because during my cadet days I knew well and favorably Colonel Poague and all three of his sons, so I asked to see a copy. Alas, my informers failed to find one, so I took up the search.

It was not until 1953 that I found the general address of the supposed owner and not until August 1954 that I made the trip from Chicago to Dallas to see her.

The original manuscript is handwritten in four ordinary notebooks about the size of those used by secretaries. It can be read without too much trouble although the reader needs some background knowledge of Virginia during the war because of numerous abbreviations of names and places. On my first visit to Texas I received permission to read and copy the manuscript.

From a careful reading of the story came my idea that it was worthy of public interest; so back to Texas I went in February, 1956, this time to obtain the original notebooks with permission and approval for publication.

Thus every reader is indebted to Mrs. Henry G. Poague and her daughter Miss Ann Poague for their generosity. To them I am personally grateful for their sympathetic understanding of my desire to honor the memory of Colonel William Thomas Poague, C. S. A., whose record as a soldier and as a citizen speaks for itself.

Mrs. and Miss Poague also placed at my disposal two photographs of Colonel Poague, the documents reproduced in the appendices and numerous other personal and official papers. These materials afford abundant evidence of Colonel Poague's distinction as an officer and his probity and standing as a citizen. All other supporting records and many illustrations have been supplied by me, with assistance from old friends mentioned in the acknowledgements.

I have also provided a map, drawn by me, of Jackson's campaigns and some explanatory notes.

Editing of the work has consisted mainly in supplying chapter headings, breaking up long paragraphs, correcting misspellings of proper names, supplying an occasional comma or period for easier reading and bringing capitalization into closer accord with modern practice. Dates of battles have also been inserted and in two instances, where Poague's memory was faulty with respect to minor detail of chronology, corrections have been made. These are the sort of changes that Poague himself would have made if he had known that publication was in prospect. No change has been made that would alter the meaning that Poague intended to convey.

Monroe F. Cockrell

Evanston, Illinois

INTRODUCTION

JENNINGS CROPPER WISE, in the preface of *The Long Arm of Lee*[1], laments the neglect of artillery in the literature of the Civil War. He attributes the slighting of this arm of the service to three principal causes: first, failure of high commanders to give ample attention to artillery in their reports; second, a tendency of writers to regard artillery as a specialty, and hence something to be avoided; and third, a general inclination on the part of persons interested in the conflict—including those who participated in it—to view it as an infantry war and to push the supporting arms into a shadowy background. After making this charge of gross neglect of Civil War gunners, Wise tends to weaken his position by citing the fame of artillery heroes. "Every Southern child," he states, "has heard, in terms of praise and tenderest affection, the story of Pegram, the youthful colonel; of the one-armed Haskell; of Latimer, the boy major; of Breathed; of Caskie; of Jimmy Thomson and Preston Chew. And lives there a son of the Southland who has not heard of Pelham, "the Gallant," so named by the lips of Lee himself?"

Even so, Wise's complaint was generally valid. And despite some correction of emphasis since publication of his work in 1915, references to artillery in writings about the Civil War tend to focus on spectacular incidents and glamorous personalities. Histories of the war and of the

---

[1] 2 vols., Lynchburg, Va., 1915, 15-16.

armies, biographies of high commanders and studies of individual campaigns give surprisingly little detail about the organization and employment of artillery. And these accounts usually afford no more than a hazy view of the everyday functions of this arm and its overall influence on the course of military events. It is not an exaggeration to state that the history of artillery in the Civil War is yet to be written.

One important thing that Wise overlooked in citing reasons for neglect of the Confederate artillery is the relative dearth of personal narratives by gunners who wore the gray. E. P. Alexander's superb account is a notable exception as are some other works well-known to specialists in Confederate history. But a glance at the bibliography of almost any comprehensive study of Confederate military operations will reveal a vast and disproportionate preponderancy of infantry and cavalry narratives.

The reminiscences of William Poague deserve special attention, then, for being the record of an artilleryman; moreover, they are the recollections and judgment of an intelligent, articulate and fair-minded man, who was in the thick of most of the big eastern battles and one who knew and had the confidence of many key personalities, including Lee, Jackson, A. P. Hill and W. N. Pendleton.

Poague wrote from memory, thirty-eight years after Appomattox. Occasionally he slips up on a name or a date, but his errors are more notable for fewness than for frequency, and all of them are minor. His mind was still alert and vigorous when he wrote, and his narrative indicated that he was familiar with official reports of battles and that he consulted such works as William

Allan's *Army of Northern Virginia in 1862,*[2] E. A.
Moore, *The Story of a Cannoneer under Stonewall
Jackson,*[3] and G. F. R. Henderson's classic biography
of Jackson.[4] Poague apparently kept no diary of his
army service but it seems reasonable to assume that while
writing his recollections he referred to the war letters
reproduced in Appendices I and II.

The reminiscences are the more valuable in that they
were written for Poague's children without any thought
of publication. Hence, there is no tendency to gloss over
weaknesses and errors of comrades high or low for fear
of damaging their reputations or offending them or their
descendants. Without so much as a waver of his pencil
he tells of his battery passing a distillery on a cold, rainy
day late in 1861, "where everybody that wanted it got a
fill of whiskey and . . . on reaching Castleman's Ferry,
we had a wagonload of drunken men—dead drunk." He
was apparently a teetotaler, as were a number of his associates, and he makes it clear that such a spree was unique
in his unit. With equal frankness, he names a notorious
Lexington, Virginia, bully as a coward and tells how he
fled from the field at Malvern Hill, despite Poague's
efforts to restrain him, crying "them bombs busted right
at my head and I'm nearly killed."

Poague does not hesitate to pass adverse judgment
on some of the higher-ups. He blames Beauregard for
failure to follow up the victory at First Manassas and
criticizes Longstreet for dragging his feet at Gettysburg.
On the whole his estimate of Jackson is high, but he is
forthright in declaring the Romney campaign of January,
1862, a failure, and to register disapproval of G. F. R.

---

[2]Cambridge, Mass., 1892.
[3]Lynchburg, Va., 1910.
[4]*Stonewall Jackson and the American Civil War* (2 vols., London and
New York, 1898).

Henderson's attempt to prove it a success. For some unaccountable reason, he makes no comment at all about Jackson's subnormal performance in the Seven Days' Campaign.

Poague has kind words for "Old Penn" (W. N.) Pendleton, his battery commander at the beginning of the conflict, and for Lee he reveals nothing but ever-increasing respect and admiration. Of Lee's majestic demeanor during the crisis at Petersburg, just before Appomattox, Poague wrote: "[His] appearance and manner were in no way different under the trying situation from what was habitual with him, except that his face was somewhat flushed. I and some other officers were amazed that he could personally give detailed instructions to so many officers. . . . Dignified, serene, self-possessed, he appeared greater than ever before. I had seen him often in battle, had interviews with him under tremendous stress, but nothing before had so impressed me with his towering greatness."

The close-up, vividly sketched glimpses of Lee, Jackson and other leaders that sprinkle Poague's narrative add much to its interest and help make it of unusual value to historians. One of his favorite subjects was the eccentric and caustic D. H. Hill, whom he had known at Washington College, and whom he encountered at Malvern Hill, sitting with leg thrown over saddle pommel, talking with General Whiting, both officers nonchalantly puffing away on cigars as they planned a desperate assault on the Federal lines. Poague tells with obvious relish of Hill's endorsing a bugler's application for a furlough: "Respectfully forwarded—disapproved —shooters before tooters." Another delightful peep at the high brass shows General Mahone during the retreat to Appomattox "sheltering himself under a poplar tree from a passing thunder shower, and in a towering passion abusing and swearing at the Yankees, who he had just learned had that morning captured his headquarters wagon and his cow, saying it was a most serious loss, for he was not able, in the delicate condition of his health, to eat anything but tea and crackers and fresh milk."

Poague's attention is by no means confined to the generals. He has much to say about battalion and battery officers—what they were like and how they conducted themselves in and out of combat. He tells of Pelham, as a lieutenant at First Manassas, stopping during a hasty withdrawal and wheeling his guns into position with the remark, "I'll be dogged if I'm going any further back"; of Ashby sitting in his shirt-tail in a Charleston hotel in November, 1861, to receive orders for an impending fight, and next day, while the battle raged furiously, walking "with arms folded apparently enjoying a quiet promenade . . . a man of the coolest courage and the finest nerve I ever knew;" of Major Shoemaker and Lieutenant Billy Williamson, engaging in a verbal joust at Second Manassas because of a misunderstanding— "two deaf men swearing at each other and not knowing exactly what the other was saying."

Some of Poague's best stories are about the enlisted men. One anecdote tells of an ambulance driver, John L. Moore, after a shell struck the tree that was shielding him "tearing back down the hill, both hands clasping his head and hollering, 'I'm killed! I'm killed!' " though the injury was relatively slight. Another choice tale is about a soldier at Fredericksburg stretched out behind a stump seeking refuge from a storm of shells. When a comrade, noting that the man's nose was within a foot of a pile of offal, called out "look at that stuff near your face," he received the retort: "Pshaw, go away! it smells like a rose."

Yet another incident, though not of a humorous slant, points up the ability of combat soldiers to insulate themselves against the horrors of war. "After the fight [Bristoe Station] was over," Poague relates, "our men got to chasing and catching rabbits, of which there were great numbers all about. Burying comrades and running rabbits at the same time! Such is war!"

Most of Poague's service was as a battery and battalion commander. The insight which he gives into the activities and problems of unit command on those levels, changes in organization and equipment, and the actual role of artillery in battle is perhaps the most outstanding contribution of his account to that tremendous mass of writing that comprises the literature of the Lost Cause.

* * * * * *

The author of this fascinating and revealing account was born on December 20, 1835, near Falling Spring Church in Rockbridge County, Virginia. His parents were John Barclay and Elizabeth Stuart Paxton Poague, middle-class rural folk who owned a few slaves, lived generously but unostentatiously and enjoyed the respect of their neighbors. Like many people of their time and station, they attached great importance to religion and education. This emphasis was manifested in the upbringing of their two sons, William and James.

William T. Poague graduated from Washington College (which later became Washington and Lee) in 1857. He then completed his law course in a school run by Judge Brockenbrough. In the spring of 1860 he hung out his shingle at St. Joseph, Missouri, but he found both the law, as practiced in that city, and the climate uncongenial.

William T. Poague leading the guns, Matthew, Mark, Luke, and John, of his old battery, May 10, 1913, at the Virginia Military Institute, in connection with ceremonies marking retirement of the guns from use by the Cadets. Accompanying the guns were members of the V.M.I. Cadet Corps. The third Cadet Captain in the line is Henry G. Poague, son of William T. Poague.

—Courtesy Colonel William Couper

The Cadet Battery on the V.M.I. Campus

The men who manned these guns during the war called them Matthew, Mark, Luke, and John, "because they spoke a powerful language." In this picture, taken in 1954, the guns stand at the base of Stonewall Jackson's statue. A plaque nearby tells how the guns—smooth-bore six-pounders of especially light cast—arrived at V.M.I. in June 1848. During the war they were used by the Rockbridge Artillery and other units until superseded by heavier guns. They were in Richmond when that city fell and were captured by the Federals. They were returned to V.M.I. in 1874 where they were again used by the Cadets until May 10, 1913. The plaque also quotes the statement made by Stonewall Jackson on May 2, 1863: "THE [VIRGINIA MILITARY] INSTITUTE WILL BE HEARD FROM TODAY."

So, in December, 1860, he returned to his native state where he went into partnership with James W. Massie, a leading attorney of Lexington.

When the war broke out, James, a medical student at the University of Virginia, immediately enlisted in the Rockbridge "Dragoons," but William, who was then 25, was persuaded by his law partner to postpone volunteering for a short time. Before the end of April,[5] he had enlisted in the Rockbridge Artillery, whose first captain was the Reverend William N. Pendleton, and whose initial equipment included four six-pounders that had comprised the Cadet Battery at Virginia Military Institute. The soldiers who manned these six-pounders in the war named them Matthew, Mark, Luke and John, "because they spoke a powerful language."[6]

When, in accordance with the usual procedure, the volunteers elected officers, Poague was chosen junior second lieutenant. A short time later, in May, 1861, the battery moved to Harper's Ferry, where it became part of Jackson's brigade, a unit which was destined to be immortalized as the "Stonewall Brigade," than which there was no more distinguished in the Confederate Army.

After participating in minor action in the Shenandoah Valley, the battery had its real baptism of fire at First Manassas on July 21, 1861. Poague was promoted to first lieutenant on August 14, 1861, and to captain on April 22, 1862. On receipt of his captain's bars (which in the Confederate Army numbered three), if not before, Poague succeeded to command of the Rockbridge Artil-

---

[5]Poague's service record in the National Archives, a copy of which was obtained through the courtesy of Robert S. Henry, shows the date of his official enrolment as April 29, and in the grade of junior second lieutenant. But Poague's account indicates that his service actually began about a week before, and that prior to the election of officers, his status was that of an enlisted man.

[6]Colonel William Couper, *One Hundred Years at V. M. I.* (4 vols., 1939) III, 304-307.

lery (it appears in official organizational charts as the
"1st Rockbridge Battery") known successively as
Pendleton's, McLaughlin's, Poague's and Graham's "company." Poague commanded the battery for about a year,
leading it with distinction through Jackson's famous
Valley Campaign, the Seven Days, Second Manassas,
Sharpsburg, and Fredericksburg, and thus helped the unit
win the well-deserved reputation as one of the very best
batteries in the Army of Northern Virginia.

Poague's outstanding performance did not escape the
notice of his superiors. On February 11, 1863, William N.
Pendleton, his first captain, but now Chief of Artillery of
the Army of Northern Virginia, in a letter to Lee sug-
gesting promotion of various artillery officers, wrote:
"Captain Poague of Virginia . . . is a superior officer
whose services have been scarcely surpassed. He has been
recommended for promotion, and should justly receive
it."[7] And Poague was the only one of six battery
commanders in Brown's battalion whom Pendleton
recommended for advancement.

Poague became a major on April 18, 1863. The
recognition was gratifying as were the many expressions
of admiration and affection from the men, with whom he
had shared so many perils and hardships, as they stepped
up to bid him farewell. Recalling the occasion forty years
afterward, he wrote: "I was deeply moved by the
unexpected character of my parting with the old battery,
and I still cherish the remembrance of it as one of the
happiest hours of my life."

Poague's first assignment as major was as assistant
to D. G. McIntosh, commander of a battalion which,
along with the one to which the 1st Rockbridge Battery

---

[7] *War of the Rebellion: Official Records of the Union and Confederate Armies* (128 vols., Washington 1880-1901) ser. 1, XXV, pt. 2, 617, cited hereafter as *O.R.*

belonged, comprised the reserve artillery of Jackson's corps. In this capacity he served through Chancellorsville.

In the general reorganization that followed Jackson's death, Poague acquired a battalion of his own, consisting of two batteries of North Carolinians (Albermarle and Charlotte), one of Mississippians (Madison) and one of Virginians (Warrenton).[8] The guns for the most part were 3-inch rifles and Napoleons. He commanded this battalion for the remainder of the war.

Poague and a portion of his command—his were the only guns brought in for the purpose from other corps by E. P. Alexander, First Corps Chief of Artillery —were posted out in front of the infantry on the third day at Gettysburg, to help prepare for and cover Pickett's charge.[9] He saw Lee several times during the three days, was much impressed by "Marse Robert's" anxiety, and was put through a pointed and embarrassing interrogation by the army commander on the afternoon of the second day after making a vague report about the presence of a moving column far to his right.

Early in 1864 Poague was promoted to lieutenant colonel. In the Wilderness fighting on May 6, 1864, during the critical period just before Longstreet arrived, when Wilcox's and Heth's divisions broke under Hancock's overpowering attack, Poague's battalion covered itself with glory and helped save Lee's army from destruction. Jennings Cropper Wise, in describing this action, states:

> [Poague's] single battalion of artillery, . . . stood alone like a wall of flame across the enemy's path. Not until the great masses of Hancock's troops came face to face with the artillery did they cease to press

---

[8] Wise, *The Long Arm of Lee*, II, 566, 568.
[9] D. S. Freeman, *R. E. Lee* (4 vols. New York, 1934-1935) III, 109; *Lee's Lieutenants* (3 vols., New York, 1942-1944) III, 159.

forward but no troops could pass through such a storm of fire as that which Poague now opened upon them. The gunners worked with almost superhuman energy, the muzzles belched their withering blasts, the twelve pieces blended their discharges in one continuous roar, and there among them stood beneath the dense canopy of smoke, which hovered above the four batteries, Lee himself as if with a halo of war above his head. The great commander knew then full well that between him and disaster Poague's battalion stood alone. What glory for a soldier! This single incident brought more of honor to the little colonel of artillery than most soldiers attain in a life of service. It would be hard for some to imagine in those soft, mild eyes, so familiar to the writer, the light which must have radiated from them as he stood among his guns on the 6th of May, 1864, the bulwark of Lee's defense, and in the very presence of his immortal commander.[10]

Poague is exceedingly modest in relating his part in the Wilderness battle and says not a word about the panic of the infantrymen. But Lee and Pendleton must have been greatly impressed by his magnificent performance. For, during the retreat to Appomattox, Poague was entrusted with the most critical artillery missions. And, in the words of Wise, "the gallant little hero of the Wilderness fully satisfied the confidence reposed in him."[11]

After the war Poague established and directed schools in the Fancy Hill community and at Lynchburg. He served Rockbridge County in the lower house of the Virginia Legislature for three sessions in 1871-1873. He served as a trustee of Washington and Lee from 1865 to 1885.

On January 30, 1885, without seeking the position,

---

[10]Wise, *The Long Arm of Lee* II, 767.
[11]*Ibid.*, 939.

he became Treasurer of the Virginia Military Institute, which position he held until retirement in 1913. He was a beloved and respected member of the college staff and the Lexington Community. He served as an elder of the Lexington Presbyterian Church from March 17, 1890, until his death.

In the years following the war Poague's former comrades twitted him considerably about his bachelor status. But he resisted all their efforts to get him into the marital fold until December 26, 1878, when at 43, he married Sarah Josephine Moore. To him and Sarah four children were born: Elizabeth Moore, Robert Barclay, William Thomas, Jr., and Henry Grigsby.

Poague died on September 8, 1914, at 78, and was buried in the same cemetery at Lexington where reposed Stonewall Jackson and many others who in the South's, and Virginia's and their time of greatness had been thrilled by the wild yells of Rebs on a charge, by the ominous whine of minie balls, and some of them, at least, by the deafening but welcome thunder of the Rockbridge Artillery.

*   *   *   *   *

What sort of an officer and person was the author of these reminiscences? He was not a large man, and those who knew him after the war were much impressed by his mildness. But his slightness of frame and his gentle ways in tranquil times did not mean that he was incapable of firmness, and even severity, when occasion required. He was unquestionably a demanding officer. The admiring Jennings Cropper Wise, in characterizing certain artillerymen who had won distinction by the close of 1862, refers to Poague as "stern."[12] and Poague's reminiscences indi-

---

[12]Wise, *The Long Arm of Lee*, I, 326.

cate that he was fully aware of his strictness as a disciplinarian. He thought the men resented his rigid control, and some of them did; but the majority apparently accepted his firmness as necessary, and admired him for the character and courage which he demonstrated in discharging his responsibilities. The esteem in which he was held was plainly manifested when he bade his battery goodbye in 1863 and when he parted with his battalion at Appomattox.

A revealing insight into the manner in which his men regarded him is afforded by a letter written to him on October 30, 1865 by Joe T. Lipscomb of Vernon, Mississippi, formerly of the Madison Battery:

> Col. you know you used to fight us *mighty* hard. I have heard it whispered in camp that you wanted to get the starch out of our shirts. I think you succeeded, particularly in the last campaign. But, notwithstanding your *fondness* for ordering the whole Madison Arty to the front, there was not a man in the whole company who did not respect you as a patriot and gentleman.[13]

Poague's influence over his men, and his effectiveness as a commander is attested by the consistently high morale of his unit. Letters of Poague to his mother, written in the last dark winter, when defection was common and desertion rampant, indicate that the spirit of his men remained strong and that they responded readily to the calls of duty.[14]

Another of Poague's outstanding traits was a deep and abiding faith in God. His reminiscences reveal a profound interest in religion, and his war letters indicate that reliance on Providence combined with a strong sense

---

13MS. This letter is reproduced in Appendix III.
14See especially letter to his mother of March 17, 1865, in Appendix II.

of duty to prepare him for the ordeal of battle and to sustain his spirit during periods of adversity. On December 29, 1864, he wrote his mother:

> I hope, mother, you will not allow yourself undue trouble about the unfavorable aspect of affairs. I meet with some who are considerably cast down. For myself, while I cannot but regret our misfortune in the field, yet I am not disheartened. Nor do I suffer myself unduly to grieve over them. First, they are not beyond remedy, and even if they were I feel that I am not responsible, for I think I have done all I could. And if one does his duty, he can leave the results with God, feeling sure that for himself all things will be done well and wisely.[15]

His religiousness apparently did not make him intolerant of those who did not measure up to his high standards of conduct. He was not a prude. His memoirs indicate that during periods of quiescence on the battle front, he participated freely in the gaiety which characterized life in the Old Dominion. He had a streak of seriousness, but he was also blessed with a sense of humor and endowed with a capacity to enjoy life.

He was valiant, honest, dependable and unassuming. And these qualities shine through as he recounts his war experiences for his children. His reminiscences derive much of their value from his being the solid sort of character that he was.

Credit for discovering the existence of Poague's reminiscences and tracking them down belongs to the editor, Monroe F. Cockrell, who is well known to students of the Confederacy for his excellent historical maps, his special investigations of various aspects of the war, his insatiable curiosity about elusive details, and his good-

---

[15]This letter is reproduced in full in Appendix II.

natured but searching letters to authors who have strayed
from the path of strict accuracy. I am indebted to him for
valuable assistance in collecting material for my own
books, and much of the information for this introduction
was gleaned by him from scattered sources. He also dug
up many of the illustrations and the material reproduced in the appendices. Without his persistent and
indefatigable effort, this book could not have become a
reality.

                                     Bell Irvin Wiley
Emory University

GUNNER
with STONEWALL

LAWYER TO LIEUTENANT

IN THE EARLY SPRING of 1860 I located in St. Joseph, Missouri, to practice Law, having just completed the course (one year) at Judge Brokenbrough's Law School at Lexington, Virginia, and passed my examinations before three judges. St. Joe was a stirring border town of about twelve thousand people, a majority being of Southern sympathies. Many excellent families and single gentlemen, some indifferent ones, many adventurers and a lot of "toughs" made up the population. It was the starting point of the Pony Express for Frisco, and the outfitting place for Western emigrants and miners— especially those aiming for Pike's Peak. The political atmosphere was getting warm and in the following November, when Lincoln was elected President, was at white heat. He received between four and five hundred votes in the city. To not a few it was evident there would be strife between the North and the South. A number of young men, myself among them, determined to return to our native states and there be ready for the impending struggle.

1

Without regard to the impending war, I had made up my mind to leave St. Joe but had not settled on a location except Southward on account of climate. The competition in that city was of such a character that I could not hope to succeed without adopting the methods of the great majority of the lawyers. Only a few men of pre-eminent abilities could afford to ignore the tricks, shortcuts and unprofessional methods of the majority. A man of ordinary attainments had to adopt them or starve. Hence, I determined to seek more favorable conditions. After the war, my health being much impaired by chills and fever which clung to me for ten or fifteen years, I gave up all idea of the legal profession and lived at the old Homestead, near Falling Spring. It fell to my lot also to care for our mother—your Grandma Poague. On January 30, 1885, without my seeking the place, I became Treasurer of the Virginia Military Institute where I am now, February 24, 1903.

On reaching home late in December I found the people not stirred up as they were in St. Joe. The great majority believed the two sections would not come to blows, that an adjustment would be reached and the danger averted. Soon after getting home I accepted the offer of a partnership with James W. Massie of Lexington, a prominent lawyer, and a Breckinridge Democrat. I had in the West supported and voted for John Bell, the Democratic Union Candidate. Rockbridge sentiment was against secession. She sent two Union Democrats to the convention.

But when Lincoln called on all the non-seceding states—Virginia among the number—for troops to force back into the Union the states that had seceded, there was at once a complete change of sentiment. Our people did not stop half way and try to maintain a neutral position, but Virginia with a unanimity almost entire, east of the Alleghany mountains, took her stand in front of her Southern sisters to resist the invader of her soil. In Lexington where the lines between the Unionist and the Secessionists were so broadly marked, where party feeling ran high and where serious clashes were with difficulty prevented, all differences forever disappeared as soon as the news of Lincoln's call for troops reached the town. The same change took place at once all over Rockbridge and throughout the state.

Two volunteer companies, the Rockbridge Rifles and Rockbridge Dragoons—organized in November, 1859, soon after John Brown's attempt to incite the negroes to insurrection—were at once called into service, and proceeded to Harper's Ferry. My brother James, a medical student at the University of Virginia, left his books and went with his company, the "Dragoons." I wanted to join his company, but was prevailed on by my partner, Colonel Massie, to remain and look after our business, who said that he, having been an active supporter and advocate of Breckinridge, felt it to be his duty to go into military service at once. He believed there would be but little fighting if any; that at the last moment a satisfactory adjustment would be found; and that his absence would be of short duration. Many of our leading men fell into the same error. The average politicians and newspapers on both sides misjudged the signs of the times and made the same mistake, believing that the great mass of the people would rise up at the critical moment and compel a peaceable settlement of our differences and thus avert the threatening clash.

The biographies of Mr. Lincoln are wide of the mark in saying that the masses of the Southern people were forced into the war by the secession leaders. It was

the act of Mr. Lincoln and his party that precipitated the
conflict which many think was inevitable. Had he not
made war upon the South, Virginia would not have left
the Union. He and his advisers managed affairs so as to
compel South Carolina to fire the first gun. The North
was the aggressor. The South resisted her invaders.
History will vindicate her course.

After our two volunteer companies and the corps of
cadets under "Old Jack" left, our people set about forming other companies, and by April 21, 1861, in three days
time, the Rockbridge Artillery of seventy men was organized. Officers were elected by the men. My friends nom-
inated me for both the 1st and 2nd lieutenancy, but I
refused to allow my name to be used. For the junior 2nd
lieutenant I was prevailed upon by my friend, Samuel C.
Smith, to allow my name to be placed in nomination and
was elected over two competitors, James Cole Davis, a
young lawyer, and John B. Craig, a noted bully and street
fighter. In the election, which was *viva voce,* Davis voted
for Craig and I voted for Davis. In the war Davis was a
gallant soldier, brave as the bravest, though not very
popular. I had the pleasure, upon his application to me,
afterwards of recommending him for the captaincy of a
negro company when it was proposed to enlist negroes.

Craig could not stand the racket of battle. I tried to
stop him from running away at Malvern Hill, when he
shouted, "Them bombs busted right at my head and I'm
nearly killed!" but he kept going.

I did not want an office in the company simply
because I was not qualified for it. Afterwards I keenly
felt my deficiencies. With a military training, I would
have been more useful in the service. In the ranks of such
a company as ours came to be, I am sure I would have had
a better time than as an officer. The very best young men

in the state flocked to the company. They were attracted, I think, by the fact that a West Point graduate, the Reverend William N. Pendleton, was our captain in the early days of the war. Those brought by his influence afterwards induced others of the same character to join us. We thus had the very best material for a battery—men who knew how to manage and take care of the horses and educated, high spirited men for the guns. Farmers, mechanics, merchants, laborers, lawyers, university students and theological students, made up the bulk of the company.

CHAPTER 2

FIRST BATTLES UNDER JACKSON

ABOUT THE 11TH DAY OF MAY, 1861, we went to Harper's Ferry where Colonel T. J. Jackson was in command. He organized the 1st Brigade, consisting of the 2nd, 4th, 5th, and 27th Virginia Infantry Regiments, and the Rockbridge Artillery. The 33rd Virginia was added to the brigade after 1st Manassas although it had been for sometime with Jackson and was virtually a part of the brigade from the first. We had many alarms but no fighting at Harper's Ferry. Then General Joe Johnston was assigned to command and Jackson took command of the 1st Brigade. Johnston's fine military judgment was shown in his giving up Harper's Ferry as untenable. It had been Jackson's purpose to hold it. After events proved the former to be correct, Johnston sent Jackson below Martinsburg to watch Patterson's army, reported to be preparing to cross the Potomac, which it did in a few days. Jackson took one regiment and one of our guns and met the advance near Hainesville (or Falling Waters), and held them in check several hours. Here the first shot in the Shenandoah Valley from a cannon was fired by our gun.

The impression made was wonderful, exciting various emotions and creating an intense desire to see and take part in the fight. A solemn apprehension arose that here at last was the reality, about which we had been thinking, talking and speculating. An almost uncontrollable impulse urged us to dash down that stone pike to the help of our comrades. A curious mental exaltation seized us; an inward questioning as to whether it was all a dream. But then came another boom from our gun! And another! Presently a limping man supported by a comrade comes: *blood* dripping from his sleeve! Yes, the war is on!

A story got afloat and is now in some books that in this affair our captain's first command was, "Aim at their knees and may the Lord have mercy on their souls, fire!" *Not so.*

After a few weeks Johnston took his little army over to Manassas to help Beauregard. Here we had a battle sure enough. Early on the morning of July 21, 1861, our battery was hitched up and waiting not far from the railroad crossing at Bull Run. Occasional shells pass over our heads hurting nobody—only frightening some of our horses. Musketry and cannonading begin up Bull Run to our left, constantly increasing. A messenger from Johnston and Beauregard on a little knoll nearby comes to our captain, who at once throws the battery into column and orders, "Trot, March," and away we go in the direction of the heavy firing on the left. And what an inspiring spectacle—that race to the battle—"Old Penn,"[1]

---

[1]This was the Reverend William Nelson Pendleton, previously mentioned by Poague. He graduated from the U. S. Military Academy, fifth in his class, in 1830 but resigned from the army in 1833 and five years later was ordained a priest in the Episcopal Church. In 1853 he became rector of Grace Church,

as our captain was called, in front bobbing up and down
on his old roan—the roughest horse in the battery, sometimes trotting, sometimes in a gallop—his saber whirling
about in every direction. At times all the teams in a
gallop—men holding on to the chests for dear life.

Johnston and Beauregard with their staffs, pass us
in a sweeping gallop; a terrific roar of cannon and musketry is heard in front; wounded and stragglers come
creeping along to the rear, dodging into the fence corners
to avoid our battery in its headlong rush. The smoke of
the battle rises above the tree tops, and with it all comes
a wild and joyous exhilaration. Oh what an experience!
Nothing ever equalled it afterwards. At last we proceed
at a walk up an incline through scattering pines, horses
blown and tired; and with shells exploding and minnies
whistling all about us, we reach the field. Our guns are
placed in line with some others already at work and we
take up our part in the awful drama.

Mine was a minor part, to look after the caissons—
they were right behind their respective pieces. I had
nothing to do and so had time to look about. After we
had been firing a little while I noticed one of our guns
standing idle behind the line of battle and not unlimbered. I looked up our captain and asked if it ought not
to be at work. "Yes," said he, "and you go and see if you
can put it in somewhere."

The guns just at this point were somewhat crowded,
but I found a position some distance to the right, where
it was placed and where it did good work. Sergeant
J. C. Davis was in charge of it.

Lexington, Virginia, which position he held for the remainder of his life, save
for four years spent in active service in the Army of Northern Virginia. He
was promoted colonel in July, 1861, brigadier general in April, 1862, and later
became Chief of Artillery, Army of Northern Virginia. See Allan Johnson and
Dumas Malone, eds., *Dictionary of American Biography* (20 vols., New York,
1928-1936) XIV, 423-455. Cited hereafter as D. A. B.

A pine tree was torn open by a solid shot near Tom Martin, an Irishman, who exclaimed, "Be jabers! Abe Lincoln's at his old trade of making rails."

After a while, perhaps two hours, our guns and others in line with us were withdrawn to the ridge on which the Lewis house stood. As we limbered up and began to leave, the Stonewall Brigade, which lay behind us, advanced to the charge, stooping forward as if to get close to the enemy before being seen.

I was riding at the rear of the battery in column and behind me came Alburtis' guns in charge of a young officer. Just as we reached the top of the ridge next to Bull Run, he exclaimed, "I'll be dogged if I'm going any further back," and wheeled his guns into battery. From reading the reports of the battle I find that these guns performed most valuable service in stopping the advance of a Federal brigade up the hollow from the direction of Bull Run; for if unchecked it would have gotten right in rear of our line of battle as it was struggling to hold on to Henry House plateau. I have also learned beyond a doubt that this young officer was Lieutenant John Pelham, afterwards the most distinguished artillery officer in the Army of Northern Virginia. He had been assigned to Alburtis' Battery as drill master and was in command of the battery that day.

Our battery stopped near the Lewis House; from this point we witnessed the retreating enemy near Stone Bridge and a Parrott rifle shot from that vicinity killed a mounted officer near us. We all saw the ricochet shot as it came towards him. Here we saw President Davis on horseback, with a stove pipe hat on. While here I went to the hollow between us and the battlefield in search of water.

Here I saw hundreds of stragglers with guns in their

hands and came up with General T. J. Jackson urging
the officers to form the men into line. After they had been
gotten into some sort of order General Jackson called out,
pointing to the edge of the pines up at the battle field,
"Now men, if you see any Yankees come out of those
pines, give them ———pepper," and wheeled his horse
towards the battlefield. A great guffaw broke forth at
his peculiar kind of swearing, and instantly turning in
his saddle, he shouted back in his shrill voice "and salt
too."

Why was the artillery withdrawn at the moment of
the charge by the brigade and by whose order? I have
not been able to find out. If by Jackson, for what purpose?
Nothing like it occurred in any of his battles afterwards.
He always fought his artillery to the very last. At Kernstown he withdrew it evidently to save it from the enemy.
Even then he fought one section to the last moment losing
one of the pieces. Perhaps and probably he feared he
might be forced to give up the Henry House ridge or
plateau. In that event he would have something on which
to rally his brigade.

That morning I could scarcely manage my high
spirited young mare and with difficulty kept her from
running away with me. After the battle I could scarcely
get her out of a walk; her ears were flapping about like
a mule's, utterly collapsed. Next day was awfully
gloomy. It was raining most of the time in torrents. I
was sent with a detail to the battle field to gather up the
captured guns and harness. In my rounds I came upon
many a friend and acquaintance, stiff in death, with
whom as boys I had gone to school and college. Jim
McCorkle, I discovered under a low bush, lying on his
back, with a note addressed to his wife pinned to his
shirt front. He was one of a number of young men of my

acquaintance who fell on that bloody field. One could hardly imagine a greater contrast in every respect between that day and the day before.

You may want to know how I felt in this my first battle. I was at no time frightened, nor was I excited after we reached the battle line. I was conscious of being in danger, but right there I felt was the place where I ought to be. The thought repeatedly came to me that I was in the hands of a kind heavenly Father, and that His merciful care and protection were over me. With all this was a most novel sensation, hard to describe, a sort of warm, pleasing glow enveloping the chest and head with an effect something like entrancing music in a dream. My observing, thinking and reasoning faculties were normal.

Afterwards for years might be heard reflections on our captain, but I think they were unjust. He certainly took us into the fight, and I interviewed him once during the fight right on the line of battle. Most of the time I was with McLaughlin, whose bearing was superb, standing between his guns giving directions and watching the effect of the shots. The responsibility for not getting more out of this victory rests mainly I think on General Beauregard. A careful reading of the reports of both sides has brought me to this conclusion.

On the 23rd I was taken sick, and but for the care and efforts of my friend, Dr. John Leyburn, I am almost sure I would not have survived the attack of typhoid fever that followed. In the face of great difficulties he put me on board a train and charged me not to stop short of home, if possible to get there. I was very sick, delirious part of the time. By watchful care of Dr. Morgan, and the good nursing of father, mother and Griffin Harvey (the black servant whom you all remember) I was raised up by God's blessing and enabled to rejoin the battery in October. A singular effect of the fever was impaired memory. I recognized my friends and acquaintances of the battery but could not recall the names of many of them. This failure of memory was gradually relieved, but I am inclined to think it has never been as good as before that terrible attack of fever.

The day we crossed the Blue Ridge was cold with a drizzling rain. A distillery was passed where everybody that wanted it got a fill of whiskey and canteens filled also. On reaching Castleman's Ferry, we had a wagonload of drunken men—dead drunk. I never saw the like before or since.

In November, 1861, the battery was sent to Jackson at Winchester. Early in December I was sent with two Parrott rifles (of those captured at First Manassas) to report to Colonel Turner Ashby at Charlestown. The order came about sundown and was urgent. We reached the town some time in the night. I learned that Ashby was at the hotel. He sent for me to come to his room, where I found him sitting up in his bed with nothing but a red flannel shirt on. He was a slender, swarthy man with long black mustache and whiskers. He was very kind in his greeting and was sorry I had to make the march by night. He directed that we find a camp and make ourselves as comfortable as possible, saying he would want us next day.

So next day we went with him accompanied by a small force of cavalry—one company, I think—to the neighborhood of the Potomac above Harper's Ferry. Here we witnessed one of those daring exploits so frequent in his brilliant career. He had learned of a boast of a party of Yankees stationed across the river that they intended to bag Ashby on his rounds along the Potomac.

He selected about 20 men and concealing the rest with our guns behind the crest of the ridge, at the head of his squad and mounted on his superb black stallion, he swooped down on a house about a half mile from the river. In a short while, he rode leisurely back with a bunch of blue coats as prisoners; their comrades on the other side looked on unable to help them. After throwing some shells into their camp causing a general stampede much to the amusement of Ashby's men, we moved on up the river but found no enemy except one or two small picket forces on the other side. Affairs of this sort were of very frequent occurrence.

Not long after, perhaps two weeks, we were with Ashby in an affair in which the Yankees got the better of us. Our battery was ordered to the neighborhood of Dam Number 5 which Jackson wanted to destroy. One of Chew's and one of our guns were placed on the hill overlooking the dam to set afire if possible the brick house on the other side from which Yankee sharpshooters annoyed our men at the dam. After a few shots they ran from the house like rats and while we were enjoying the sport, all at once a full battery opened on us from a wooded hill across the river. They had our range from the first and threw their shells right among us. Our captain, McLaughlin, ordered everything to cover of some woods about 50 yards to our right, leaving the two guns standing in the open and sent me in haste to bring up the rest of our guns. The enemy never stopped firing.

On my return with the guns up a long ridge a little to the right of the enemy's line of fire, I saw on my left in a great hollow or sinkhole Chew's team with limber wrapped around some saplings, and hung fast, and old Jack doing his best to get the drivers and men out from behind logs and trees to extricate the team and limber.

Not a man stirred from cover, under the awful fire the Yanks kept up. As I moved by the general called to me and I halted. As he approached he called out, "Mr. Poague, can't you come and get those men and horses out of that place?" My reply in substance was, I didn't think I could if he couldn't. "Well," said he, "fetch your guns on to top of the hill."

We soon found ourselves under fire, for the enemy seemed to be searching the whole region with his fire. Jackson was afoot and right in front and now and then would duck his head as shells came near. As we neared the top of the ridge we found every man and officer behind a big tree and all dodging first to one side and then to the other, Captain McLaughlin and Colonel J. T. L. Preston being as nimble as any of the lot. Jackson did not take to a tree, but occasionally bowed to those infernal shells.

Did I dodge? Yes: just as low as my saddle pommel would allow. But who was that man out there walking slowly back and forth near the deserted guns in the open field, with arms folded apparently enjoying a quiet promenade, totally indifferent to the hellish fire raining all about him. That was Turner Ashby—a man of the coolest courage and finest nerve I ever knew or saw in the Army. Well, just as we got to the place where I expected to be put to work, the enemy suddenly stopped, *and we didn't open.*

The author of this demoralization we learned was Best's Battery. We got a chance afterwards to get even with him.

I saw Jackson afterwards in every one of his fights, big and little, but never detected the quiver of a muscle.

CHAPTER 3

TRIAL AND TRIUMPH IN THE VALLEY

NEXT CAME THE ROMNEY CAMPAIGN (January 1862), which on account of the extreme cold and the snow and the rain was simply terrible—terrible in the sufferings of man and beast, in demoralization of a great part of the army and in the number of deaths that followed, and all without any substantial fruits. But for the weather, I believe General Jackson would have achieved brilliant results. But he seemed to leave the winter out of his calculations, or else thought he could conquer the elements. Colonel G. F. R. Henderson, his accomplished biographer, labors to prove the campaign a success on the whole. But it would not require one to have taken part in that expedition to be convinced that it was far from being a success. He has only to read the official reports to be forced to admit that it was a failure.

The great Napoleon was no match for hoary winter. General Lee's plans and efforts in West Virginia were not successful because of bad weather and roads.

Hooker[1] (who as a soldier, however, is not to be named along side of Jackson) started on a winter campaign from Fredericksburg, but did not get out of sight of his camp before he was forced to abandon it. Jackson had been disappointed in not getting his promised reinforcements earlier in the season, and when they did arrive, rather than give up his plans determined to take the chances of the weather, and it all went against him. On this expedition he shelled the town of Hancock across the Potomac, after having demanded the surrender of the Federal force occupying it, and giving two hours in which to remove women and children. It was Sunday and our battery did the bombarding. Some of the men ducked their heads and dodged as the shells passed, but this was the last of such performances as Dam Number 5 witnessed the first.

It was in this affair that John L. Moore, the ambulance driver, came to the top of the ridge where we were firing to take a look at things, stationing himself 50 yards to left of battery and behind a tall, slim, dead locust tree. It wasn't long before a stray shot coming towards him caused him to lean close to the sapling. The shot struck the tree about ten feet above his head. Old John L. was knocked into a dazed condition and went tearing back down the hill, both hands clasping his head and hollering, "I'm killed! I'm killed!" It must have been a terrific blow, for he was laid up for some time with a swelled face and head. But we couldn't help laughing as he went down that hill seemingly twenty feet at a jump and "killed."

Jackson went back to Unger's Cross Roads on the way, as we thought, to Winchester. Here many got fur-

---

[1]Poague should have written Burnside, as the reference obviously is to Burnside's famous "Mud March" of January, 1863.

loughs, men and officers, Captain McLaughlin among the latter. Then I was left in command of the battery. In a few days it was reported that Kelly had evacuated Romney, and immediately the whole army marched thither. I suppose we (our brigade) were there about 10 or 15 days when we were ordered to vicinity of Winchester where we went into winter quarters.

While at Romney General Jackson issued an order for the artillery officers to turn over to the quartermaster their riding horses (they had used government horses hitherto, with the sanction of the authorities). This would have put all of us on foot with snow and mud nearly knee deep. I went to see the general about it, who kindly suspended the order until the officers could provide themselves with mounts.

We had a most dreadfully disagreeable time at Romney. Our large company was quartered in a small church, Methodist I think, and had to do our cooking in the graveyard, which nearly surrounded the church. It rained and snowed almost the whole time. Horses tied to the hitching rope had to eat what little feed they got in the mud. No boxes or nosebags were to be had. The mud was so deep that they could with difficulty change their position. The men soon became infested with vermin. We officers escaped by occupying the high pulpit. The situation was disgusting.

At last an order came to follow the Brigade. This we did with great delight along the Winchester Turnpike and through a heavy fall of snow. Our camp that night was in the woods with the snow scraped away for our little tent and a roaring fire in front. We had a fairly good supper and a sound sleep in the fresh air and clean surroundings; the horses also ate and rested in some comfort. This was paradise compared with our miserable plight in Romney.

In all the war I never had a similar experience—never endured such physical and mental suffering as on this trip. The expedition seemed to everybody to be a dismal failure. Our confidence in our leader was sorely tried. Loring's part of the army was in a state of semi-mutiny, and Jackson was hissed and hooted at as he passed them. This I had from a friend in the Georgia regiment who teased me a great deal about the "crazy general from Lexington."

The next time I met him—Captain E. P. Howell of Atlanta—he was a most enthusiastic admirer of "the great 'Stonewall'."[2]

About February 1st (1862) I got a furlough and while enjoying myself as only a soldier can when at his home on furlough, I received an extension of my leave and an order to procure recruits for the Artillery. About March 15th I took about sixty men to Jackson's army then camped near Edinburg, Shenandoah County. Here I had my first and last fight with "gray backs" (vermin). I went to a creek on a cold windy day, took off my new flannel underwear, sunk it with rocks in the cold water, washed myself clean, put on new flannels intending to return in a day or two to get my shirt and drawers—minus the little creatures as I hoped; but an order to hitch up and move at once left me no time to look after them and I saw them no more forever.

Then came on the battle of Kernstown (March 23, 1862), where our battery of six guns did good work. At the close of the fight as our troops were forced back, I was directed to take a position with my section and to

---

2After the war Howell became editor and co-owner of the Atlanta *Constitution*, and made it one of the country's best newspapers. Henry W. Grady and Joel Chandler Harris were among his assistants. *D. A. B.*, IX, 301-302.

hold the advancing enemy in check as long as possible, to
cover the retreat of our men. This we did in our front,
until flanked on both sides. Several of our horses had been
wounded and in withdrawing through the woods down
the side of the ridge, the off wheel horse of one gun was
killed and fell across the pole. While trying to extricate
the dead horse the Yanks came on us. Seeing there was
no chance to swap horses, I ordered the men to quickly
unhitch and mount the other horses. The gun was lost,
and men and horses barely saved. Under cover of the fast
falling darkness we got out of the terrific fire pouring
upon us, caught up with the other pieces and ere long
reached the rest of the battery passing to the left of a
pond or lake, and soon reached the pike. We learned that
nearly all who went to the right of the pond were captured. The enemy made a feeble pursuit. Had "Old Jack"
commanded on the other side he would have pressed
forward and doubtless gobbled up a big lot of us.

Next day our battery was part of Jackson's rear
guard. We had a brush with enemy's advance at Cedar
Creek; thereafter they gave us little trouble. While
exchanging shots across Cedar Creek one of their shells
passed high over our battery, fell far to the rear in the
middle of the pike and exploded in the midst of the 27th
Regiment, killing several men and wounding others. This
was the only damage done us on the retreat and by a
stray shot, the regiment being out of sight and behind the
hill from which we were firing.

At Rood's Hill where we stopped some days, our
new brigade commander, General Charles S. Winder,
paid our camp a visit and hauled our captain over the
coals for the way he allowed the horses to be picketed—
ropes down in the mud, some horses astride and others
tangled up. McLaughlin thought it a pretty good joke on

his lieutenants, but they thought he was the man that got
the roasting.

Jackson put General Garnett under arrest for withdrawing the Brigade too soon at Kernstown. All the
regimental commanders approved Garnett's course.
Jackson preferred charges.

Colonel Grigsby told me after the war that the
charge was in substance inefficiency in deploying and
managing his regiments on the battlefield, and not pre-
mature retreat, as we all understood at the time. Jackson
asked all of his colonels of the Stonewall Brigade if they
could not have held their positions longer, at least until
reinforcements reached them. Their replies were in the
negative.

Captain John Carpenter relates the following: That
night his company were strung down the pike near
Middletown cooking. In his mess was a young moun-
taineer, who, as he espied General Jackson passing, asked
him to share their supper which was about ready. Jackson
thanked him and said he believed he would. As he was
sitting on some rails beside this fellow and apparently
relishing the frugal meal and enjoying the warmth of the
blazing rail fire, the boy, who was not over stocked with
bashfulness, spoke up: "General, it looks like you cut
off more tobacco today than you could chew." Jackson
smiled and simply said, "Oh, I think we did very well."

As we passed the little branch where my flannels
were submerged, I went after them, but they were gone.
The army left the pike near Harrisonburg, crossed the
Shenandoah at Conrad's Store and went (April 19, 1862)
into camp at mouth of Swift Run Gap. Here took place
the reorganization by the election of regimental and
battery officers. The wisdom of this procedure has been
much questioned. Officers who had tried to keep up di..

cipline were not popular and failed of reelection. A few were on the other extreme and hence not reelected.

Our company had men enough for three batteries and was to form a battalion with McLaughlin in command as major. I understood this arrangement to be approved by General Jackson. About 240 men were present. Two new companies were organized, with Arch Graham captain of one and J. Cole Davis of the other. The expected order from the War Department authorizing a battalion was not received. The original company then elected officers, with myself captain and Arch Graham, William M. Brown and J. C. Davis as lieutenants. I never felt myself qualified for the command of such a splendid body of men, but as I seemed to be so considered by them, I accepted the responsible position.

In less than six months many of them were dissatisfied because they thought me too strict. When I took command the discipline was poor. I was given to understand by the new brigadier that I would be held strictly responsible for the condition of the battery in every respect. I had to see that there was no ground for the charge of partiality by the plain uneducated men. I had to require better attention to the horses. I had to haul up many delinquents in petty matters. I was directed to prefer charges of desertion against some who over-stayed their leaves. In fact, our new brigadier required the regulations of war to be carried out in every particular.

All this seemed very hard to our men who had had a pretty easy time as to discipline. Consequently I was much disliked by some and hated by a few. The majority approved of my administration, and I had many warm friends. They recognized the difficulties of my position and made allowance for my failures and defects. All the men knew I would not shirk danger, and that I would not needlessly sacrifice them. So that, on the whole, I managed to get along fairly well. This much I feel I ought to tell you about my position in the company.

Jackson's next fight was at McDowell (May 8, 1862). Not a single cannon shot from our side. Artillery could not be gotten to the top of the mountain where the infantry had a hot time.

Next day the enemy under Milroy was pursued to the neighborhood of Franklin in Pendleton County. The next day we rested, it being the Sabbath. Major Dabney (the Reverend R. L. Dabney) preached to a large congregation in a beautiful meadow.

I have been told it was on this expedition that three prominent citizens of Lexington wishing to learn something of Jackson's proposed route deputed one of their number to interview him on the subject. To his query Jackson replied: "Judge B——, can you keep a secret?" "Most certainly," said the judge. "So can I," replied old Jack.

On returning to the Valley we crossed Massanutten Mountain, marched to Front Royal (May 23, 1862) where Bank's outpost was stirred up, routed and captured. Early next morning I was ordered to report with two guns to Ashby on the road from Front Royal across to Middletown. Dick Taylor's splendid Louisiana Regiment was also going that road. I came up with Ashby and his cavalry not far from Middletown. He soon brushed away the enemy's picket and almost before they knew it, we burst upon Bank's column in retreat toward Winchester. A few shots from Chew's and our guns scattered them in every direction and then such a time as we had running them along the pike. Their teamsters abandoned wagons and for two miles or more they lined the road. Most of the horses were taken from them. Their infantry and cavalry disappeared, where, no one could tell.

Only once did they make a stand and as we unlimbered at the top of a little rise in the road, a whole regiment rose up as if out of the ground (they had been lying concealed in tall grass or grain) and cleared out down the road instead of giving us fight, and gobbling us up, for we hadn't a single infantryman or horseman to support us, except Ashby himself. His cavalry were looting wagons and capturing horses, utterly undisciplined. This was Ashby's weak point. Not a man of our guns was out of place. They only peeped into the wagons and picked up a few oil cloths and blankets of the hundreds scattered along the road. The only living thing found was a negro baby in a wagon.

After this race of six miles we found at New Town a regiment or two and a battery drawn up for a fight. This stopped us a while, until the rest of my guns got up, when we lit into the battery and drove it away about sundown. I learned that it was Best's, the same that made it so hot for us at Dam Number 5.

General Jackson having come up with Stonewall Brigade, the retreating Yanks were pressed nearly all night. Occasionally they checked us a bit but they would soon be on the run. He kept our battery right at the head of his column next to his small cavalry force. Once the cavalry ran into an ambuscade and came tearing back and got tangled up with our teams, our men having to jump in among guns and caissons to keep from being run down. "Old Jack" halted about 2:00 A. M. near Winchester and let us have a short nap.

We started at daybreak and soon came up with Yanks posted about Winchester (May 25, 1862). As we were getting into position on the ridge to the left of the pike, we were set upon by both infantry and artillery at 300 or 400 yards, an ugly predicament truly. But we managed to change position under this hot fire and got a less exposed location, to which we held on until the enemy were flanked out by Taylor's Louisiana Brigade. See his account of our behavior here, in his book styled *Destruction and Reconstruction*.[8]

A wheel of one of the guns got jammed behind a big white oak gate post in changing our position. Some of the horses being shot, I ordered the rest to be quickly unhitched and with the cannoneers to get back under cover of ridge. That gate post had to be gotten out of the way before the gun could be extricated. A call for a volunteer was responded to by Corporal A. S. Whitt, who took an axe and screening himself, as well as he could, behind the gate post and the fence and on his knees chopped the big tough post more than half off when he was relieved by Corporal William Strickler who finished it. Strange to say, neither was touched in the fusillade kept up on them. It being down grade the gun was easily run by hand to a place in line with the others and put to work.

Needing more men I sent back to the section in reserve for four men. All promptly came to the firing line except Jonathan Agnor who squatted in the grass about 100 yards in rear. My attention being called to him, I rode down and ordered him to one of the guns. Before he reached the piece, he was killed. After the war his old father complained bitterly of my having caused his son's death as he regarded it, but the facts were just as I stated.

The enemy was soon routed and driven pell mell

---

[8]See Richard Taylor, *Destruction and Reconstruction* (New York, 1879), 56-59.

through Winchester. As we followed close in pursuit the old men, the women and the children lined the sidewalks cheering, shouting, laughing and crying. It was a scene never to be forgotten. Jackson pursued a few miles with his infantry and artillery but not as fast as the enemy ran, when we stopped and went into bivouac to rest. A brigade of cavalry under a good leader would have captured many more prisoners than we did.

At this place I wrote my first report on my knee, and a very meager lifeless thing it was. I supposed that after the brigade commander saw and read it, the fire would receive it. But lo and behold, I find several of my very imperfect reports published in the Rebellion Records, as the U. S. Government calls the volumes.[4] I ought to have embraced in them many things that were a part of the history of the battery and that would have reflected credit on the men. I find that many reports were so written, and if you make a comparative estimate of the services of our battery along with some others as based upon the reports of the commanding officer, ours would suffer by the comparison.

After a day or so of rest Jackson sent the 1st Brigade to the vicinity of Harper's Ferry. The few Yanks encountered were soon brushed away and then suddenly near Hall Town we turned about and made a notable march back through Winchester and on by Strasburg, near which we learned the hitherto unexplained reason for our rapid march, as we beheld the smoke and heard the booming of cannon out towards the North Mountain. It was Fremont trying to break in upon Jackson's retreating column. Much of the time in the march to Port Republic, our battery was part of Jackson's rear guard, in which

---

[4]Poague's report of the Winchester battle, May 25, 1862, is in *O. R.*, ser. 1, XII, pt. 1, 761-762.

position we had several combats but the battery invariably held its ground until ready to move. The cavalry was once stampeded and ran through us.

At Port Republic the battery did its share of good work both Sunday and Monday (June 8-9, 1862). Read Colonel William Allan's account in his book[5] of an incident at the Port Republic bridge on Sunday. I never saw Jackson as much stirred up at any other time. He had just made a narrow escape from capture personally and he did not know what force Shields was pushing to his rear. His first and only words, as he reached our battery, which was the nearest force to the bridge, were: "Have the guns hitched up, have the guns hitched up!" He was addressing no one in particular. Galloping on to the infantry he almost shouted: "Have the long roll beat, have the long roll beat!" Returning from brigade headquarters where I had reported to General Winder what I had heard from a cavalryman as he passed me in a headlong race to Jackson's quarters in the town about Shields' army coming up the river, I met "Old Jack," who snapped out, "Captain, have your battery ready at once." On replying that I had already given orders to hitch up, he said: "Good, I will be with you presently." And so presently he led us to the field overlooking the bridge, when we went to work as related by Colonel Allan.

Our firing that day along with other batteries upon Shields' columns of infantry as they marched up the river road to Port Republic was unusually accurate and very destructive. Without a shot from Jackson's infantry, Shields' brigades were broken up by artillery alone and driven back down the river in considerable confusion until hidden by the friendly forests of the Lewis estate. Next day in Shields' onslaught upon Jackson's left, they

[5]*The Army of Northern Virginia in 1862.*

got one of our guns, a brass six-pounder. The horses were shot and as the brigade was forced back the gun had to be abandoned. The enemy seemed to prize this gun highly, for in their disorderly retreat a couple of hours afterwards, they managed to get the gun away.

That night (June 9, 1862) we bivouacked on top of Blue Ridge in Brown's Gap with nothing to eat but tough flap jacks, the toughest I ever tackled. Lieutenant Davis, though badly shot in the body by a minnie, managed to ride his horse to the top of the mountain that night. In a day or two we were camped right over Weyer's Cave. Fremont and Shields had skedaddled down the valley and next day I was ordered to the vicinity of Staunton to rest and refit.

We settled down in a beautiful timothy field belonging to Hugh W. Sheffy. He fussed with me about trespassing on his fine grass, but as I had been located there by the post quartermaster, he let me alone and fell to berating the quartermaster, giving me to understand that that individual was unfriendly to him and that was why we had been put on him. But before we had time to rest or to begin to refit, suddenly an order came to me to march in the direction of Charlottesville. This ordering the battery to rest and refit at Staunton was to deceive the people as to his plans, evidently, as we have since had reason to believe.

CHAPTER 4

SEVEN DAYS THROUGH SECOND MANASSAS

WE DID NOT GET into the first day's fight at Richmond
with our brigade, though very close to the combatants.
The continuous and tremendous roar of musketry that
evening exceeded anything I heard during the war. Next
day we occupied the field of Cold Harbor overlooking
Grapevine Bridge. Here General Lee, followed by well
mounted and well dressed staff, rode up to the battery
and asked for Private Robert Lee. He could not be found
for sometime. At last some one found him asleep under a
caisson. As he came up to the general, blinking and
rubbing his eyes and as dirty as he well could be, the
general broke into a broad smile, saying, "Why Robert,
I scarcely knew you, you've changed so much in appearance." The staff all grinned and tittered and all of us
greatly enjoyed the interview between the splendid looking, handsomely mounted general and his son. If you
had looked the company over, you could not have found
a more unkempt and "ornery" looking Reb than Bob Lee,
Junior. But he was as good a soldier and as fine a fellow
as any in that splendid company.

This was the first time we saw General Lee and there was something about him that impressed me as no other officer did except Joseph E. Johnston. Here we first saw a balloon used by the enemy, and my first emotion was one of contemptuous indignation for the unfair advantage they thus sought, but I soon got over this, as I reflected that all things are fair in war.

At White Oak Swamp we had an indecisive duel with the Federal artillery. At Malvern Hill (July 1, 1862) we were engaged in a terrific fight with their batteries and an idea somehow got abroad that our artillery was ordered to retire from the field. One battery did leave in unseemly haste, and this made things look panicky, but the men of our battery didn't budge an inch, and we continued the fight along with some other guns until the enemy ceased. On this occasion as previously stated, John Craig, a blustering bully on the streets of Lexington, couldn't stand the racket and broke for the rear.

While in position here, Captain Carpenter of the Allegheny Roughs and I received a message from General Jackson to come at once to where he was, and on reaching him we were introduced by him to Generals D. H. Hill and Whiting. Jackson stated that General Hill wanted a couple of batteries that he could depend on, and remarked to General Hill: "These two officers command batteries that you can depend on."

Old D. H. was sitting with leg thrown over the pommel chatting with Whiting and both smoking cigars. They were planning a desperate assault to the right of Jackson's position. A most perilous part was assigned us in the attack and we were conducted to the woods in rear of Hill's line and then directed to await orders from him. But the orders, if sent, never reached us, and we had to endure the most trying of ordeals standing idle under

a terrific fire. As commanding officers, Carpenter and
I were much perplexed and worried and heard nothing
from him until late in the afternoon and then simply,
"Rejoin your command."

In this battle a shot from a gunboat went through
an oak 30 inches in diameter and took off the head of one
of my men, John Brown, of our ambulance force, 400
yards in rear of the battery. That night we went into
bivouac a mile or two in rear of the battlefield, with
orders to hitch up at 3:00 A.M. and be ready to move. I
had to hunt around and rouse the men next morning by
shaking them; and one man I had to kick pretty severely
but failed to stir him. He was dead—one of the enemy.
Daylight revealed that we had slept where a fight had
taken place.

Next day we marched towards Harrison's Landing
where McClellan took shelter under his gunboats. Without attacking him the army returned in a few days to the
vicinity of Richmond. While on the march to Harrison's
Landing "Old Jack" received his first ovation from the
Army of Northern Virginia. Cheering began far behind
us, so far away that we scarcely heard it, increasing until
in tremendous volume it swept by us with Stonewall
bareheaded on Little Sorrel at his best speed, the staff
strung out away behind, doing their level best to keep
up, until gradually the cheering died away in the distance
far ahead. Little Sorrel was a pacer and could make a
mile in about 2-40 and whenever we saw him it was at
this tremendous stride or in a slow lazy walk.

Speaking of pacing reminds me that Jackson when
at the Institute reported Cadet David S. Hounshell for
not trotting at artillery drill. His answer to the report
was, "Can't trot, am a natural pacer."

By the way, Hounshell was far better known to us

boys at college than was "Old Jack." The former was noted for his backwoods style of oratory, and was always called on with vociferous cries at debating society celebrations and never failed to respond. He was also a noted fighter at the Institute. If we had been called on at that time to say which of these two would be best known in the future, I really believe the majority would have said the chances were in favor of Hounshell. But what a mistake. The one known and admired the world over, the other never heard of.[1]

D. H. Hill was Professor of Mathematics at Washington College, Lexington, Virginia, in 1853-54, his last and my first year at the college. When he heard my name he asked if I was the boy he knew at college and on my answering affirmatively, said he was glad to see one of his pupils, but little did he think our meeting again would be under such circumstances. He was brave, a stubborn fighter, extremely sarcastic, disposed to make light of the other arms of service—cavalry and artillery—and bitter towards "Yankees" as he usually termed them. On an application from a member of a band for a furlough he endorsed: "Respectfully forwarded, disapproved — shooters before tooters." Yet he was especially careful —more so than any officer of his rank—to commend officer and private for good conduct in battle, but he peppered shirkers and cowards. When near Drewry's Bluff in June, 1864, under Beauregard, he did not hesitate to criticize General Lee in a note to Beauregard; a rare bird was old D. H.

While encamped near Richmond for some days, my father along with some of our old neighbors made a visit to our camp, bringing good things to eat, etc., which, of

---

[1]Hounshell, a prominent lawyer, practiced before the Supreme Court of the U. S., and served as Colonel, First Battalion, Virginia State Line, C. S. A.

course, were greatly enjoyed after our strenuous campaign in the Valley and about Richmond. He was greatly gratified to find me a captain and commanding such a remarkably fine company. My first handsome Confederate uniform was a present from him at this time. These were the halcyon days of Jackson's troops. Well earned rest, good rations, abundant supplies from their valley homes, proximity to the capital with its varied attractions, the praises and admiration of its people for Stonewall and his followers all combined to make it most pleasantly remembered ever afterwards.

In the midst of this happiness and enjoyment Jackson was sent to Gordonsville to look after Pope. While in camp here near the village, I had my first experience of the troubles and difficulties of a commanding officer. Under stringent orders from brigade commander General Winder I had to place under arrest several men of the battery and prefer charges for desertion; that is, absence without leave, which offense in its most serious forms under the regulations of war was considered as little different from desertion. They became greatly incensed at me as if I had initiated the disciplinary action and as if I ought to or could have prevented it. One of them, a member of a prominent family, became so offensive and insulting that it was with the greatest difficulty that I controlled my temper and prevented a personal altercation, which I thought he wanted to bring on.

Then there were minor matters of administration and discipline that could not be overlooked, but which had not been enforced by my predecessor. So I soon found myself getting unpopular with a certain class of men. This, of course, was not pleasant. My position was a trying one, and my ambition for promotion not sufficient to make me unwilling to exchange with a private in the ranks, but a certain sort of pride held me to my work. After a while these things ceased to worry as I became more and more assured of the respect and confidence of a large majority of the men.

Our next fight was at Cedar Mountain (August 9, 1862) where at one time we were on the edge of a serious disaster, threatened by the enemy passing through an unoccupied part of our line in the woods to the right of the main road, and taking our troops in the rear. Our first position was just on the right of the road, one gun being stationed in it. Had we remained here we would have been destroyed or captured. But fortunately the guns had been moved some 400 or 500 yards to the right to get a better chance at a Yankee battery which had been annoying us, one shot from which had killed our brigade commander, General Winder, right beside my left gun.

In the confusion that ensued from this rear attack, my guns were rendered useless, being surrounded by our infantry and all we could do was to try to rally the infantry and restore order, for it was on the verge of a panic. At this junction "Old Jack" appeared and by his example and exertions, mainly, and with the help of the regimental and brigade commanders, order was restored and the enemy driven from the woods. In the melee the most conspicuous persons, as I remember it, were General Jackson, General W. B. Taliaferro and David Barton, a private in our battery.

While this was going on at the road, the Stonewall Brigade under Colonel Ronald, Winder's successor, was further to our left, driving the enemy before them. I have tried by reading the reports of this battle to fix the responsibility for this gap in our line, through which the enemy penetrated to our rear, but I find no data upon which to fasten it on any subordinate officer. The interval was between the 2nd brigade and the 1st or Stonewall Brigade and was in the dense woods where it could not be observed. I am inclined to think it lay between the 1st brigade commander and the army commander; or possibly Winder's fall had something to do with it.

In this battle our artillery contributed its full share to the final victory. Latimer's battery[2] was posted upon the side of Slaughter Mountain at least a mile to my right and commanded a large portion of the enemy's left and greatly annoyed them, especially their artillery. From the report of one of the Yankee battery commanders I learn that they suffered much from the fire of our battery.

My published report is a meager affair, as indeed were all my accounts that have survived. But, then, the battery did not require the reports of its commanders to help make and maintain its reputation. General A. P. Hill's report contains strictures on the Stonewall Brigade undeserved and unjust. I can't help thinking he was a little jealous of "Old Jack" and the old Stonewall Brigade.[3]

Our next campaign was under General Lee against Pope, and with Jackson the battery went on his famous march to Pope's rear at Manassas, after having been engaged in a number of combats along the Rappahannock. That march through the beautiful Piedmont section— who can ever forget, that was along? The fine weather, magnificent country, the mysterious march, through fields and byways, the unknown destination, the possible collision at any moment with the enemy, the sight of the Bull Run mountains and then the stealthy approach upon

---

[2]The battery commanded by Joseph W. Latimer, the famous boy major, schooled at V. M. I. He was in the Seven Days' battles and was mortally wounded at Gettysburg.

[3]Poague's report of the battle of Cedar Mountain is in *O. R.* ser. 1, XII, pt. 2, 213; A. P. Hill's report is in *ibid,* 214-216.

Manassas—all served to keep us intensely interested and all the time on the *qui vive.* The whole situation intensified with the consciousness of tremendous risk to be followed by tremendous possible results.

The morning of the 28th of August (1862) found us at Manassas Junction which had been captured by our cavalry before daylight. Immense stores of all kinds had been collected here. Every Confederate got more than he could eat and carry away, and the rest was destroyed. While we were all sprawled out on the grass, resting and sleeping, a Yankee infantry brigade under a General Taylor marched up along the railroad from Bull Run, passed the artillery without firing a shot, although within a hundred yards of us, but did not quite reach the station before they were discovered by our infantry and by them driven back across Bull Run. I did not fully understand the situation at first and did not open fire on them until they had passed in their attack upon the Junction. The artillery peppered them with canister in their retreat and followed them to Bull Run. "Old Jack" kept along with our guns and repeatedly waved his handkerchief calling on them to surrender. But they did not hear him, nor did they stop to fire on us. The whole brigade ought to have been bagged, but managed to get away without serious loss.

In this affair an amusing thing occurred. Billy Williamson, a former member of the battery but then a lieutenant of engineers, happened to fall in with us on this trip and with my permission was in his old place at one of the guns doing his best, as he always did. He was quite deaf and so was our chief of artillery, Major Shoemaker. Williamson failed to hear an order of Shoemaker and did not obey him, whereupon Shoemaker shouted out his order with an oath and Williamson cussed back at him and told him he was a commissioned officer and he must mind how he talked to him. "Well, then, if you are an officer serving with this battery, then I place you under arrest," said Shoemaker. "Very well," replied Williamson. "I'll see you after we get through this affair," and so both went about their duties. After the fight was over, Shoemaker came to me and asked who that fellow was that refused to obey his orders and was so insolent in his reply to him. I explained the situation telling him he was very deaf and did not hear his order probably. "You say he's deaf? Well, then, that makes it all right. Send for him and I'll release him from arrest and apologize," and so he did. Those who were nearby and heard them said it was ridiculously funny, two deaf men swearing at each other and not knowing exactly what the other was saying.

About the time some of our company took possession of a deserted sutler's wagon, up rode Captain von Borcke of Stuart's staff and claimed it for the cavalry. A pretty warm dispute ensued, when the captain with some impatience appealed to me exclaiming, "Captain, just let me get in and see if there is anything I need, and then your men can have the whole store." This was agreed to and presently the gigantic Prussian emerged with a box of cigars apparently well satisfied with that as his share. Our fellows helped themselves to a great variety of things and to my lot fell the most useful thing I could have desired— a little mattress made of best quality rubber cloth and cork shavings, the very thing for sleeping on the wet ground. It had on it the name of Major Buck, New Jersey Volunteers.

During the night we marched by the light of burning cars and storehouses towards the old battlefield of July 21, '61, which we crossed about daylight. Halted near the well-known storehouse on the Warrenton pike, then about noon moved to Sudley Mills and then to near Groveton (August 28, 1862) where we (Jackson's Army) had a hot stand-up fight with the enemy, who thus prevented the breaking of his column as it moved on the pike towards Centreville. The conflict was at close quarters, neither line yielding, with heavy loss on both sides—the dead all in a line. Night ended the strife and the Yanks stole quietly away and next day Jackson had his force posted along an unfinished railroad nearly parallel with Warrenton pike, the Stonewall Brigade occupying the now famous cut on the right of his line. Our battery was not in line, but standing in rear of the brigade some 300 or 400 yards near some haystacks—a narrow strip of woods being between us and our brigade. All hands were lying around the stacks resting and sleeping, "Old Jack" himself with his back against a stack taking a nap.

Suddenly a rattle of musketry broke forth at the cut and along the line to the left, arousing everybody. Jackson, telling me to hold the battery in readiness and await orders, quickly mounted his horse and went towards the firing. Shortly a Yankee battery appeared to our right on the plateau overlooking Groveton, and went into battery, flanking Jackson's line of battle. I at once moved the battery several hundred yards out into the fields and somewhat on the flank of the enemy's battery. We soon diverted his attention from our infantry and got into a lively fight which resulted in his being driven from his position with a gun disabled and left on the field.

In this affair my horse was shot under me. Sergeant Dick Paine, a capital soldier, having been mortally wounded, I mounted his little black mare which I rode until after Sharpsburg when I supplied myself with a fairly good sorrel horse. Soon after this I was posted along with one other battery on the plateau from which the battery had been driven and from this excellent position contributed our share in repelling the assaults made on Jackson's position on that day as well as on the third day's battle (August 30, 1862), where we were joined by Longstreet's artillery under Stephen D. Lee.

From reading some accounts of this great battle, some who did not know all the facts would conclude that only Longstreet's artillery was engaged in smashing up the Federal lines as they advanced to attack Jackson on the third day. I have an impression at least that the Rockbridge Battery and several others of Jackson's batteries had a hand in that business.

After the repulse of the last assault and as Longstreet's infantry in full view from our position made the grand and decisive charge on the enemy's left, our chief, Major Shoemaker, couldn't resist the temptation to have a hand in that part of the fray, and so selecting some four guns from Jackson's various batteries on that plateau, and putting me in command of all the rest with instructions to hold our position until further orders, went thundering along down the pike, pitching into every body of Yankees he could come up with, for the enemy's right was now retreating, until he was stopped by an officer from Longstreet to know who he was and by whose orders he was pushing so far in advance. I was told that Shoemaker was somewhat nettled and replied, "I am under nobody's orders in particular but can't he see I am helping to run them damned Yankees to Washington?" I joined him about dark near Stone Bridge where we went into bivouac.

The night of the second day when all was quiet I took a cup of genuine coffee with Colonel Baylor, commanding the brigade, and afterwards attended a little prayer meeting held by the college boys, among them Captain Hugh White. It was my last meeting with these two model soldiers. Both fell next day near the cut.

After the last repulse of the enemy at the cut, I rode a short distance in front of Jackson's right and found the enemy's dead so thickly strewn that I could not ride among the silent ranks. Near the edge of the cut, a Federal soldier by a convulsive movement got nearly to his feet, not uttering a word or a cry—a part of his head actually torn away—and then fell prone upon the ground. I instantly found myself seized with an almost uncontrollable impulse to end his apparent agony with my pistol. Here, as on other fields, I experienced most divers and conflicting emotions—sincere sympathy for individual suffering and wishing I could give relief, and an inner rejoicing and intense satisfaction at the sight of hundreds of my country's foes deliberately put to death.

In this battle was an occurrence that tested the quality of our men. While firing from the ridge on the third day, a Parrott shell from the enemy came tumbling along the ground right toward one of my guns and when within 30 or 40 feet it was seen to be smoking. On it came and exploded under the trail of the gun. Not a man budged from his position. Eugene Alexander fell badly wounded, losing his arm. What an honor to command such men! It was in this fight that Major Shoemaker became furious at Captain Garber of the Staunton Artillery for not trotting when commanded and threatened him with a court martial, but nothing ever came of it. When asked by Major Shoemaker about it, I told him Captain Garber was not to blame I thought, and that Jehu himself could not have forced those jaded horses out of a walk.

The second day our battery turned loose on a brigade

of the enemy that had secured a position threatening Jackson's right and drove it off when "Old Jack" rode up and said, "good morning Captain, that was handsomely done."

A few days afterwards we were engaged at Ox Hill (September 1, 1862) during a heavy thunder storm, results indecisive, except to still further demoralize the enemy, who were now exerting every effort to get under cover of the fortifications at Washington. In the affair at Ox Hill General Kearny of the Federal army rode up to our lines, turned and as he galloped off lying prone on his horse's neck, was killed. No trace of wound was to be found, the bullet having entered the anus.

Lee on Traveller at Rockbridge Baths, near Lexington, Va., 1866
Photograph by A. H. Plecker of Lynchburg

This is the picture of which Meredith, *Face of Robert E. Lee* states (p. 76): "The one not shown is one of those that Traveller's restiveness spoiled; moreover, the whole surface is too badly reticulated for reproduction."

D. H. Hill

"*Brave, a stubborn fighter, extremely sarcastic. . . . On an application from a member of a band for a furlough, he endorsed: 'Respectfully forwarded, disapproved . . . shooters before tooters'. . . . a rare bird was old D. H.*"

Thomas J. (Stonewall) Jackson

At First Manassas, "*General Jackson called out . . 'Now men, if you see any*"

Jackson's position near Groveton, Second Manassas

" 'Old Jack' kept along with our guns and repeatedly waved his handkerchief calling on them to surrender."

The Antietam, from Burnsides Bridge.

Antietam Creek, from Burnside's Bridge

"We were concealed in a body of small trees and they could only mark out places by the smoke rising above them. We protested against attacking such an overwhelming force. Pelham replied with a laugh, 'Oh, we must stir them up a little and slip away.' And so we did stir them up, and with a vengeance they stirred us up."

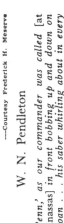

W. N. Pendleton

"*Old Penn,' as our commander was called [at First Manassas] in front bobbing up and down on his old roan . . . his saber whirling about in every direction.*"

John Pelham

"*At First Manassas, exclaimed, 'I'll be dogged if I'm going any further back', and wheeled his guns into battery.*"

Heros von Borcke

"At Second Manassas, while Poague's men were rifling a sutler store captured from the Yankees, von Borcke exclaims, 'Captain, just let me get in and see if there is anything I need, and then your men can have the whole store' . . . Presently . . . [he emerged] with a box of cigars apparently well satisfied with that as his share."

John Thompson Brown

"Colonel Brown . . . took me with him to call on the Gay Mont people. Here we found Pelham and were just beginning to have a pleasant time . . . when in steps General Rooney Lee. . . . at once it seemed as if an iceberg had floated into the room. Such frigid dignity I never encountered."

Bloody Lane, Sharpsburg

"Private Bob Lee came up and spoke to his father, and said, 'You are not going to put us in the fight again in our crippled condition, are you?' 'Yes, my son, I may need you to help drive those people away,' he replied as he pointed towards the enemy's lines."

—Sketch by A. R. Waud from "Century Magazine," issue June 1887.

Coehorn Mortars—light mortars set in wooden bed and transportable by four men—
of the type sent to Poague by Lee's order, August, 1864.

—From Miller's "The Photographic History of
The Civil War"

"I had hoped for the election of
McClellan."

—From Miller's "The Photographic History of
The Civil War"

"I fear Gen. Early doesn't pray as hard
as Stonewall Jackson did."

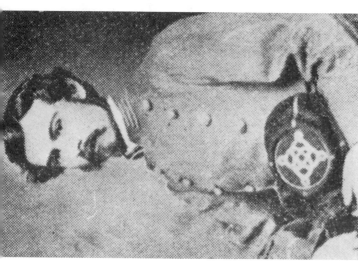

Randolph Fairfax

At Fredericksburg "two of the finest soldiers in the battery were killed nearly at the same moment—Lieutenant Baxter McCorkle and Private Randolph Fairfax. . . the former the Cavalier, the latter the Scotch-Irish—each the perfect flower of his type."

John Hampden (Ham) Chamberlayne

At Fredericksburg, a horseman reined up and "called out . . . 'good for you, we need you! We're knocked all to pieces! Whoop! Isn't this fun!' . . . Hayslett broke out . . . 'that fellow must be crazy'. . . . I replied: 'He's all right, that's Ham Chamberlayne.'"

Turner Ashby

At Harper's Ferry, "walking slowly, back and forth . . with arms folded . . . totally indifferent to the hellish fire raining all about him . . . a man of the coolest courage and finest nerve I ever knew."

Marye House, Fredericksburg

"I had it from one of our men who is good authority that a certain fellow was stretched out behind a good sized stump with his nose within twelve inches of a pile of filth, when another seeing the situation and coveting the stump for himself exclaimed, 'look at that stuff near your face.' 'Pshaw, go away! It smells sweet as a rose,' he replied."

Major William T. Poague "[At] *Hamilton's Crossing* [in April, 1863] . . . *I received official notice of my promotion to major and assignment to a battalion of which former Captain D. G. McIntosh was the senior major. . . . I was not disappointed in being the junior officer, for I had heard that McIntosh was a very fine officer and it was agreeable to me not to have the responsibility.*"

Yankee reporter's communication to Philadelphia *Inquirer,* Sept. 20, 1864, pointing up effectiveness of artillery fire of Poague's battalion. The report was clipped by C. S. Venable of Lee's staff and forwarded to Poague through his division commander, George E. Pickett.

From the James River Squadron.

Special Correspondence of the Inquirer.

UNITED STATES STEAMER "COMMODORE MORRIS," JAMES RIVER, Sept. 20th, 1864.

I was up at Dutch Gap on the 19th. Our forces are progressing finely with the canal, though the Rebel shells are flying fast. The loss of life is considerable. Our batteries cover theirs, and there is excellent firing on both sides.

From the signal station at that place Richmond can be seen and every movement of the enemy watched. The station is invaluable in directing the fire of our guns. The rams attacked the lower one yesterday afternoon, co-operating with Howlett's Battery, and the other one recently unmasked, but failed to hit it. The canal is almost through, and on a level with high water mark, so far as completed.

Deserters are coming aboard of our gunboats in considerable numbers. Fourteen in one night is a single instance.

Dunkard Church.

Dunkard Church, Sharpsburg Battlefield

"While firing from our second position just in front of Dunkard Church woods, along the left of the pike, keeping back a force of infantry, a body of enemy infantry pressed along by our right flank. . . . Fearing they would get in our rear and thus gobble us up, I galloped down into the woods to our left and front to see if I couldn't find some of our infantry."

E. P. Howell

After the Romney campaign of January, 1862, "I had it from a friend in the Georgia regiment who teased me a great deal about the 'crazy general from Lexington [that] Jackson was hissed and hooted as he passed' [the Georgians]. . . The next time I met [this Georgia friend]—Captain E. P. Howell of Atlanta—he was a most enthusiastic admirer of 'the great Stonewall'."

J. J. Pettigrew

On the march to Gettysburg "I received orders to report to General J. J. Pettigrew . . . a fine officer, polished gentleman and always handsomely dressed. . . [July 17, 1863 on the return from Gettysburg he] was slain to the great grief of the whole army."

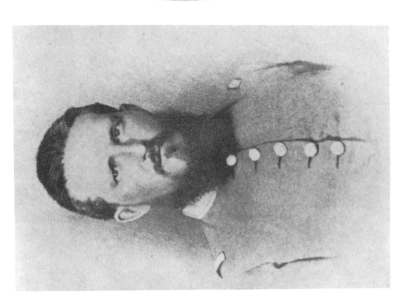

Frank Paxton

Killed at Chancellorsville, "at the head of the Stonewall Brigade in my judgement the best specimen of a Scotch-Irish soldier given by Rockbridge to our cause."

Stone in which Stonewall Jackson died

House in which Stonewall Jackson died

"In the woods nearest Chancellorsville, the slaughter was as great as I ever saw on any field."

Room in which Stonewall Jackson died

"The loss to our country and our Southland was beyond estimate."

John B. Gordon

At Appomattox, *"I reined up at Gordon's side, saluted and asked where the regiment was that was to go to Penick's relief. His face was pale and I saw that he was laboring under some overpowering emotion, as pointing to his front* [at a white flag] . . . *he said with tremulous voice and heartbroken tone 'That will stop them' and turned his face from me."*

James Longstreet

On the morning of July 2 at Gettysburg: *"General Lee called to me and asked, 'Have you seen General Longstreet or any of his troops . . . I wonder where General Longstreet can be.' "*

William Mahone

"This performance of Mahone's men [near Farmsville, April 7, 1865] *was as fine a piece of work as I ever saw. I looked up General Mahone and thanked his officers and men who so gallantly came to our aid. . . . I found him shielding himself under a poplar tree . . . swearing at the Yankees who . . . had captured his headquarters wagon and his cow."*

George E. Pickett

On July 3 at Gettysburg, as the Confederate assault on Cemetery Ridge reached the climax, *"General Pickett himself appeared on the line of my guns . . . looking intently to the front. . . . I then said, 'What do you think I ought to do . . . Our men are leaving the hill.' 'I think you had better save your guns,' was his answer and at once rode off."*

COLONEL POAGUE IN SONG AND STORY

Colonel William T. Poague, of Lexington, a famous Confederate artillery officer, is in Richmond for medical treatment. He is stopping at the home of a friend.

Colonel Poague's name appears quite frequently in Miss Mary Johnston's book, "The Long Roll." He has also figured in more than one piece of verse in recent years, extolling his merits and achievements as a gallant soldier.

On December 20, 1912, his seventy-seventh birthday, Professor Robert T. Kerlin, of the Virginia Military Institute, paid him the following poetic compliment:

Little does he resemble Mars,
Or son of Mars; no battle scars
Make grim and terrible that face
Where only kindly smiles find place;
No lightning in those mild blue eyes
But only light, you might surmise.
No giant he—about as tall
As France's Little Corporal
Or England's hero of the seas—
And of the same breed as these.

Look once again at him: 'tis worth
Your while; few such are still on earth.
Of Stonewall's Old Brigade was he,
Commander of his battery;
And Jove's own thunderbolt he hurled
Where Stonewall's standard was unfurled—
This man that rides so modestly
Each morn—aged seven and seventy—
His little sorrel down·
To his work through our town.

At Bull Run where war's tempest
    burst
Upon the land, and our mettle first
By the proud invading host was tried,
He fired the guns at Jackson's side
And helped to earn the name that
    stayed
By the famous old Brigade.
All through the Valley fights that
    brought
His Chief immortal fame he fought;
Cold Harbor then and Malvern Hill,
Antietam, fatal Chancellorsville;
In Gettysburg's most dreadful fray
He cleared for Pickett's charge the
    way,
His steady fire, with fatal aim,
Belched thunder on the foe;
Go read upon the bronze his name,
And you'll begin to know.

Look once again at him, look well;
He went through war's four years of
    hell,
And none was braver in the fight
And none to fame has better right.
His horse shot down, his hat shot
    through,
Battered and all but broken in two,
On every field he stood his ground,
And by his ready guns was found
On Appomattox' mournful day—
This hero that did wear the Gray.

William T. Poague as Treasurer of Virginia Military Institute. Photo by Miley and Son

Poetic tribute to Wm. T. Poague on the occasion of his 77th birthday.

CHAPTER 5

TO MARYLAND AND BACK

ABOUT THIS TIME Jackson issued an order forbidding men to ride on carriages or caissons. When we reached Goose Creek our chief, Shoemaker, authorized mounting the men in crossing. When we reached the Potomac, under Shoemaker's interpretation of the order, I mounted the men on the gun carriages and caissons, and as we reached the farther bank, I found Major Frank Paxton, now serving on Jackson's staff, supervising the crossing of troops. He informed me he would have to report me for violating Jackson's order. "All right," said I with a show of indifference about the matter. Next day came an order from the general placing me under arrest and quite a number of other commanders were in arrest for the same thing. We all felt secure, however, with our chief between us and "Old Jack."

We went into camp near Frederick, Maryland, but being confined to limits of camp, the situation was rather irksome. A Dutch farm house was constructively within limits, and so we captains laid claim to it under the peculiar circumstances, and got first rate meals. The inmates were not ardent Confederates, but all the same they took our Confederate money and gave us the best they had. I never enjoyed good things to eat, as much in my whole army experience, and several infantry officers having found the house a good place to board, we all had really a grand time.

The men of Jackson's command all had a good time resting and eating and many imbibing rather freely. In consequence of the latter, a sort of free fight broke out between the men of two of our batteries, Rain's and Carpenter's, which was quelled mainly by Lieutenant Baxter McCorkle of my battery, a stalwart young fellow and officer in charge that day, who knocked the brawlers right and left and soon quelled the disorders.

Private E. A. Moore tells of a ludicrous bit of experience in Frederick City. As soon as he got into the town he met Joe Shaner, the most noted forager in the battery, on his way to camp with a bag of eatables across his shoulder and a canteen of old apple jack slung around his neck. Nothing would do but Ned must have a swig right then and there. Joe objected to taking off the canteen, but he might have a drink from it as it hung. Joe being of low stature and Ned over six feet, the latter fell to his knees and pulled away at the canteen, when some fellows passing called out "just look at that old cow and calf."

In a few days Jackson's command was on the march for—nobody could guess where—his battery commanders still in arrest. Somewhere near Boonsboro I bargained with a citizen for a splendid young horse ridden by his daughter at the last fair and winning highest prize. I said if the Federal army came into that section, he would be stripped of everything, as he was known to be an ardent Southerner. The price in Confederate money was agreed on, he to deliver the horse next day at some point.

Among my friends I found money enough with what I had to comply with my contract. But I never saw or heard of the owner or the horse again.

Not knowing how long we would be under arrest, we captains petitioned General Jackson for permission to go to our wagon train, wherever it was, and get an outfit of clean underclothing as we were wretchedly dirty. The reply came at once: "You are released from arrest. Resume command of your battery." The matter was never heard of again. It was supposed that Jackson learned that we acted under implied authority of his chief of artillery.

Somewhere on this march Jackson barely missed capture by a reconnoitering detachment of Federal cavalry. The second afternoon (September 11) found us crossing the Potomac at Williamsport and that night we camped west of Martinsburg.[1] Here one of my guns under Sergeant Clem Fishburn was detached to accompany a small force to North Mountain depot to look after a body of the enemy. This gun did not rejoin the battery till after Sharpsburg, having been sent to Williamsport where it did good service in aiding to repel the enemy's cavalry.

The next morning we entered Martinsburg and found that the enemy had fled earlier in the day.[2] On the night of the 13th we were at Hall Town and the following day went with the brigade to a point near Potomac and from a hill opened fire on Bolivar Heights.

While engaged here early on the 15th I noticed on the enemy's works what I took to be a white flag and reported the fact to Colonel Grigsby commanding the brigade. He could not see it and ordered me to continue

---

[1]Poague erroneously wrote that the enemy "was driven out of Martinsburg" on this day. The Federals retired from Martinsburg early on September 12.

[2]This sentence was added by the editor to correct Poague's error in chronology.

firing. Very soon I was convinced that the white flag
meant surrender and again reported what I saw and my
conclusion. He either could not or would not see the flag,
which now looked like a small tent fly, and ordered
"d-n their eyes, give it to them." After this we fired very
slowly. After awhile here comes a courier from "Old
Jack" on the extreme right with orders to "cease firing,
enemy at Harper's Ferry has surrendered."

We afterwards learned that the commanding officer
was killed by a shell after he had capitulated. Under the
circumstances we all thought the shell went from either
our battery or Carpenter's, (or whatever battery was
engaged along with us). We remained in this position
until about dark and then were directed to go back to our
recent bivouac near Hall Town and feed men and horses,
the rations for both being green corn. In returning it got
so dark that on entering a dense wood I couldn't see my
hand before my face, and so I had to throw the reins on
the little black mare's neck (Sergeant Dick Paine's horse
before mentioned) and trust to her guidance. She
brought us right to the place we left that morning.

Some time in the night we started for Sharpsburg,
as it turned out; though, as usual, we knew not our destination. We crossed the Potomac below Boteler's Dam
near Shepherdstown about day break and proceeded to a
beautiful oak grove, covering a little vale on the left of the
pike a short distance from Shepherdstown. Here we found
a lot of infantry and were joined by other batteries and
more infantry. This was our first chance for a nap after
our first night on this trip—some 48 hours.

Some time during the day we were aroused by the
bands striking up "Dixie," accompanied by thousands of
Confederates, and such inspiring, soul-stirring music I
never heard as the volume of harmony rolled and thun-

dered through that little vale in the forest. It seemed to put new life into both men and animals and late that afternoon as we followed "Old Jack" through the village and out on the Hagerstown pike to a position beyond the Dunkard Church we felt ready for anything our beloved general might undertake.

Just at twilight I was ordered to open on a battery that was annoying our people to the right and rear of our position, and it was not long before we knocked him out. He could not get our range somehow, and overshot us. His shells were easily traced by their burning fuses from the time they left the mouth of the guns. Soon all was quiet and we retired a little distance to some straw stacks at the lower side of the woods from Dunkard Church. Our horses received a good feed of old corn and all of us obtained a good night's rest and got everything in readiness to move at dawn.

The pickets of both sides at once got to work, and soon enemy's columns were hurled against the left of the army, occupied by Jackson's men. I cannot undertake to describe the awful fight of Sharpsburg (September 17, 1862)—in my opinion the most terrific and most trying to his troops of all of Lee's battles, owing mainly to the fact of his being outnumbered $2\frac{1}{2}$ to 1 and his troops not all being up at the opening of the fight. Read Allan's excellent account of it.[3] One of the trying things was the wandering shells from the enemy's big guns on our flank from across the Antietam. Before we left our bivouac at day break, one of our men, Sam Moore, was mortally wounded by them. A fire of any sort from the rear is very disturbing and makes one feel, whenever made conscious of it by roving missiles, that the enemy are not fighting fair, but he soon gets over his irritation as he

---

[3]William Allan, *The Army of Northern Virginia in 1862*, 342-444.

remembers that he is playing a game in which all things are fair.

We fought from four different positions that day. Our first was some distance in front of Dunkard Church woods and our second at the edge of said woods, both places being left of and near Hagerstown pike. While firing from our second position just in front of Dunkard Church woods along the left of the pike, keeping back a force of infantry, a body of enemy infantry pressed along by our right flank and on the other side of pike, driving our men back towards the church. They paid no attention to our guns, although within 50 yards of us and a single company could have driven us away or captured the battery, as we had no infantry support whatever. As we were not firing at them they seemed to be willing to let us alone. Fearing they would get in our rear and thus gobble us up, I galloped down into the woods to our left and front to see if I couldn't find some of our infantry and apprise the commanding officer of the situation up at the pike. I ran across a brigade, under Colonel Billy Smith ("Extra Billy") and reported to him that our forces across the pike were being forced back and if not checked the enemy would soon be in my rear and asked what was best to be done.[4] He thought he ought to maintain his position in front of the enemy who were apparently getting ready to attack him, but for me to gallop to our retreating troops and tell them to "try and hold their own against the enemy and that I am here yet." "Well," said I to myself: "I am afraid you won't be there very long, old fellow."

When I reached our guns, I found that the enemy

4William "Extra Billy" Smith, Virginia governor and U. S. congressman before the war, was during the conflict successively a member of the Confederate congress, colonel, brigadier, major general and governor of Virginia. *D. A. B.,* XVII, 361.

were clean past us and getting into the woods in our rear. In the meantime a tremendous roar of musketry broke out at the position of old "Extra Billy" and not knowing how long he "would be there," I withdrew my guns from this position between two bodies of the enemy to a little ridge about 500 yards distant on a line with the church. Here General Jackson rode up. He approved what I had done and directed me to be in readiness to open on either body of woods. I was here not very long before "Extra Billy" and his men came back out of the woods where I had left him.

Our third position was a hill to the left of Jackson's position at beginning of battle and our fourth with one gun on extreme left of Lee's line of Cavalry near the Potomac. This last was under Major Pelham with three other guns, who, by direction of superior officers beginning with General Lee himself, was trying to see if McClellan's right could be turned. We artillery captains didn't know the object of the movement, and were disposed to criticize Pelham for turning us loose within 500 yards upon an immense battery of some thirty pieces in plain view and easily counted. Fortunately we were concealed in a body of small trees and they could only mark our places by the smoke rising above them. We protested against attacking such an overwhelming force. Pelham replied with a laugh, "Oh, we must stir them up a little and then slip away." And so we did stir them up, and with a vengeance they soon stirred us out. Pelham skilfully led us to one side out of the range of the murderous fire which was continued for some time on the place we opened from. We battery commanders thought Pelham had gotten permission to look up a fight and were down on him for what we regarded as a most indiscreet proceeding. In my report you may read between the lines my feelings.[5] But we did him injustice. We know now that General Stuart in compliance with instructions from General Lee through Jackson, took this method of determining whether McClellan's flank could be turned. I suppose Pelham knew what he was sent there for.

About 11 A.M. General Lee with some of his staff rode up to the battery and called for the commanding officer. We were in position on a slight eminence in rear of the south end of Dunkard Church woods. He wished to know the condition of the battery and its supply of ammunition. I replied that we could make out to use all three guns from our present position, but for any rapid movement only one piece was equipped, as our teams had suffered severely in the morning fights. About this time Private Bob Lee came up and spoke to his father, and said "You are not going to put us in the fight again in our crippled condition, are you?" "Yes, my son, I may need you to help to drive those people away" he replied, as he pointed towards the enemy's lines. After a few pleasant words with his son, General Lee rode away as quietly and composedly as if nothing special was going on. His equanimity and self possession under the awful stress of that fearful day were marvelous.

We bivouacked that night a little distance in rear of our line of battle. Next day was quiet and I was not called on to leave our resting place. About sunset one of Jackson's staff brought me an order from him to take a small detail and after dark to bring off a gun left on the field to right of the Dunkard Church wood and near the pike and about halfway between the pickets of both armies. If I needed more men, the officer in command of our line near the place had been instructed to furnish as

---

[5]Poague's Sharpsburg report is in *O. R.*, ser. 1, XIX, pt. 1, 1009-1010.

many as I should call for. I got a number of infantry men, and proceeded to hunt up the gun.

From our pickets I learned about where the gun was. "Right out there," said they in a whisper pointing to the front, "not more than 75 or 100 yards." The detail of infantry refused to go a step beyond the picket line. Neither persuasion nor threats made any impression on them, so I had to undertake the ticklish job with the little squad of our own men under Corporal Jack Jordan, a muscular, fearless, sensible, practical man, whose superior could not be found in Lee's army, I believe. Our trouble was to find the gun, and we began to think we had been misdirected. After groping about for some time we stumbled on it, unlimbered. Absolute silence reigned. Being somewhat bewildered by our wanderings and without landmarks to guide. None of us were quite sure as to the direction we should take; but all agreed that the gun was probably pointing towards the enemy. So, fixing things as well as could be done to prevent rattling, we stole slowly and stealthily away, now and then stopping to blow, and reached our picket line some distance from where we came through.

The infantry men were soon found, and now made no objection to hauling the piece behind our main line. According to my instructions, I turned the gun over to the officer commanding that part of the line, and thus we were done with the disagreeable and hazardous affair. I never could find out whose was the deserted gun—only that it belonged to a Georgia battery; perhaps Lane's. Nor could we understand why the owners of the gun were not required to get it off. While it was a compliment from "Old Jack" to be selected for such a delicate and risky task, we could not help feeling somewhat indignant that those who lost the gun were not required to recover it.

Next day (September 18, 1862) we crossed the Potomac into Virginia and for many weeks were camped in the beautiful lower Valley. At this time took place the reorganization of the artillery, the various batteries being detached from the infantry brigades and formed into battalions of from four to six batteries—commanded by a major or lieutenant colonel of artillery, sometimes by a colonel as was the case with the command to which we were assigned—Colonel J. Thompson Brown's Battalion, a part of what up to this time constituted the reserve artillery of Lee's army, under Brigadier-General W. N. Pendleton, our former captain. Our battery was loth to leave the old Stonewall Brigade of which it had been a part from the very beginning of the war. The friends and relatives of many of us were in that command, being from the same section of the country, the Valley of Virginia, and our whole battery was proud to be known as an integral part of that immortal brigade. To me the separation was sad and weighed on my spirits for months and only when assigned next spring as junior major to McIntosh's Battalion in which I found a Rockbridge battery and my old college friends Hale and William Houston and Dr. A. J. Hayslett, did I begin to get reconciled to the change.

Though Brown's Battalion had seen but little actual fighting it was made up of capital material and well drilled under its accomplished officers, Colonel J. Thompson Brown, a wealthy Petersburg man, and Lieutenant Colonel Lewis Coleman, Professor of Greek, University of Virginia.

I soon got to like them both and afterwards became much attached to them—pleasant, considerate, genial gentlemen, kind and just in dealing with their subordinates.

After being in the battalion some weeks Coleman one day playfully twitted me about the superior drill of the other companies (batteries) over ours—expressing surprise that a battery of the reputation of the Rockbridge Artillery should fall short in this respect. I replied by acknowledging the fact—explained it by saying that "Old Jack" had kept us so busy fighting that there was little time for drill. He accepted the explanation laughing and said, "You are excused, you are excused"—much in the fashion, I fancied, he would have treated a favorite pupil in Greek.

While in camp below Winchester I heard it was contemplated to give me promotion, but that a claim on the part of friends for promotion of some other captains of batteries, caused a postponement of the matter. I had been without a friend at court after Captain Alf. Jackson, a college mate and "frat" chum gave up his place as assistant adjutant general to "Old Jack." True, Sandy Pendleton, my day room mate at college, was there, but I could not count him as a friend, but rather against me with any influence he might have, as I learned on good authority. I could not exactly understand his attitude to me, unless it was because some of his friends in the battery had been disciplined. Anyhow my promotion did not come at that time as I and my friends had been led to expect. However it was no serious disappointment. I ought to have been contented with the command of the Rockbridge Artillery through the war, for there was no other company I knew of that would begin to measure up with it.

Well, after a most pleasant sojourn in the lower Valley, in November we crossed Blue Ridge at Thornton's Gap. Near the top we could look down and see troops moving at a number of points in opposite directions, on account of the tortuous windings of the pike. We did not stop at Fredericksburg, but our battalion (Brown's) was scattered along the Rappahannock below the city as far down as Port Royal some 20-odd miles—my battery being near the latter place. We were expected to look after the gunboats with our two 20-pounder Parrotts, given us after Sharpsburg.

CHAPTER 6

FREDERICKSBURG

ON THE 12TH OF DECEMBER Colonel Brown's orderly came to my camp about sunset with the message, "Colonel Brown sends his compliments to Captain Poague and directs him to move at once to Fredericksburg. The enemy is crossing there in force." Young Fleming's voice trembled with some sort of emotion as he delivered the order. He supposed it was intended that I should follow the river road along which Colonel Brown's and the other batteries had been stationed and would move, but said in reply to my inquiry, that the road was in very bad condition. "All right," I said, and "please present my compliments to Colonel Brown and say that I will try to be there in time for the fight."

Orders at once issued to get ready to move at a certain hour—6 o'clock. If Fleming had waited and seen the hustle and heard the jokes and the merriment and the shouts of the men as they prepared a hasty supper and packed up he might have supposed we were really anticipating a fine time on the morrow. We moved a mile or so to the forks of the road, halted while I went into a

nearby house to inquire about the roads, found the family
at supper and learned of an interior road very much better
than the one along the river, though longer. I determined
to take the inland route by a place called the Sycamores.

The name of the family I do not recall. It consisted
of a brother and two sisters, all past thirty apparently. I
asked the gentleman if he could not go with me as guide
stating that it was important to reach Fredericksburg by
daylight (December 13, 1862). He hesitated, saying it
would not do for him to leave his sisters alone, but after
a consultation with them he agreed to go. I am sure I
could not have found the way over the cross country
roads, but with his guidance, we marched briskly over
good roads and reached Hamilton's Crossing before daylight and bivouacked in a fine forest where we made
roaring fires and got a nap and breakfast.

In the meantime after our arrival the rest of the
battalion under Colonel Brown came up and stopped in
the woods near us. The colonel was much surprised and
pleased to find us ahead of him as he supposed I would
follow on the same difficult road by which he marched, he
having had an earlier start and a much shorter road. For
this expeditious night march "Old Jack" in his report
complimented the battery.[1]

In the forenoon Colonel Brown stationed the battalion behind a ridge in rear of the right of Jackson's line
of battle and awaited orders. Shortly, by his direction, I
detached Lieutenant Graham with two guns to report to
Major Pelham in the bottom to the right and front of
Hamilton's Crossing where his section fully maintained
the reputation of the battery, winning from "Glorious
Pelham" very high compliments—being much impressed
with the cool and nonchalant bearing of both Graham

---

[1]See *O. R.,* ser. 1, XXI, 633.

and his men. The casualty list of both men and horses was heavy.

Here a touching incident occurred. "Doc" Montgomery fell mortally wounded and soon Robert Fraser was badly hurt and fell near him. When Montgomery realized his hopeless condition he asked Fraser to pray for him, who suffering as he was, made fervent supplication to heaven for his friend, regardless of the terrible fire they were under. Poor Montgomery died next day in the field hospital shortly after my visit to him and after sending tender loving messages to his family.

The rest of us quietly rested in the bright, genial sunshine until about 1 P.M. when Colonel Brown was ordered to relieve Lindsay Walker's Battalion which had been badly smashed up on what was afterwards known as Dead Horse Hill. My guns were at the head of the column and with me was riding Dr. Hayslett. As we began the ascent of the hill there came tearing down through the woods towards us a horseman bareheaded with handkerchief around his forehead, a short pipe in his mouth and suddenly reining up, called out, "where are you all going?" and as I told him "to take the place of Walker's Battalion" he fairly shouted, "good for you; we need you! We're knocked all to pieces! Whoop! Isn't this fun!" As he turned his horse and galloped back, Hayslett broke out with one of his noted big laughs, "Well, that fellow must be crazy, don't you think?" I replied: "He's all right, that's Ham Chamberlayne."

Colonel Brown got all his batteries into position without trouble, the enemy having ceased bombarding that part of our line. We had a good opportunity to view the field, and never before had we seen as much infantry and artillery of the enemy at one time. After an hour or

so General Jackson in a brand-new uniform came to
where my guns were and with his glass surveyed the field
for some minutes. Then he called me to him and said,
"Captain do you see that battery at what appears to be
the junction of two roads?" at the same time pointing to
the place, which was directly in our front. I replied in
affirmation and that I had for sometime noticed it firing
at something away to my right. "Can't you silence that
battery?", he asked. "We can try General," I said. "Well
open on it," he ordered, "and if they get too hard for
you, turn your gun on their infantry and try and stampede
that!" He at once turned and went off to the left.

The order amazed me, and as I thought a moment,
I was confounded by its apparent absurdity. Stampede
infantry after being knocked out! But it was "Old Jack's"
order, exactly as he gave it,—for the words burned themselves into my memory—*never to be forgotten.* I quoted
it verbatim in my report, and was sent for by Colonel
Brown who thought I must be mistaken and that I'd
better change the phraseology. I told him I gave General
Jackson's exact words and that I preferred the report to
go up as I wrote it and that I was willing for the General
himself to see it and so no change was made and never
a word was heard about it.[2] I have told this to many
persons, perhaps every year; I have had occasion to repeat
it, and every one was mystified, but only told it to those
who knew me well enough not to doubt my veracity.

What did he mean! Well I have no trouble about
the first part, but the second part puzzled one. It must be
borne in mind that no other guns in our long line of
artillery—Brown's I mean—got any orders to open. I
think General Jackson wanted to draw the fire of the
batteries on his front with as little damage as possible to

---

[2]Poague's report of Fredericksburg could not be found in *O. R.*

his own, so that he could count and locate them and accordingly selected the two on his extreme right for the purpose. We know he designed a night attack and did carry on his plan advancing both his infantry and artillery until he satisfied himself that it was impracticable. Our battery on account of its crippled condition took no part in this attempt, but I was told by Dr. Hayslett that their battery—Captain Donald's—a little after dark moved forward, accompanied by infantry, crossed the railroad and went some distance—"Old Jack" riding near Captain Donald—until the enemy discovering the movement began to pour in a tremendous fire. Then, in obedience to General Jackson's order, Captain Donald returned. And so having this attempt in view he wanted to know the number and location of enemy's batteries.

As to the latter part of his order I never could understand it except as a bit of grim humor. He knew what would happen when we opened, about five minutes after he left. Such a tempest of shot and shell I never have witnessed any where during the war. It was as if "Old Jack" had said to the Yankee Devil, "seest thou my faithful old Stonewall battery! Do your worst and see if thou canst terrify it!" I don't know how many were the batteries in all that wide stretch of bottom that were turned loose on our devoted section. It was not long before Colonel Coleman came rushing right into the vortex of the storm demanding: "What does all this mean, Captain! Who ordered you to open fire?" "General Jackson himself" I replied. "Well, I take the responsibility of ordering you to stop," he stated. "Very well, Colonel," I responded, "those Yankees down there will pretty soon compel us to quit, anyway."

Just then it was that Colonel Coleman was cut down, receiving a wound that resulted in his death, some weeks afterwards. The order to cease firing was given, and the men directed to seek any cover they could find behind trees and logs. Two of the finest soldiers in the battery were killed nearly at the same moment—Lieutenant Baxter McCorkle and Private Randolph Fairfax; and Arthur Robinson of a prominent Baltimore family was mortally wounded. Lieutenant McCorkle was trying to extinguish fire in the leaves near the caissons when his side was torn open by a missile of some sort. Fairfax was struck by a fragment in the middle of the forehead, death following quickly. Several others were wounded more or less seriously.

Just after Colonel Coleman was struck Colonel Brown arrived to see about matters and while I was telling him, a piece of shell cut through my hat brim within an inch of my head, producing a sensation of much heat about my eyes and forehead. While still talking with him a heavy shot struck within three feet of him, but he didn't move a muscle, and was perfectly cool and self possessed in all the fiery ordeal. All of our men who saw Brown and Coleman in this first baptism of fire concluded that they were of the right stuff and "would do."

As I passed driver John Connor holding his lead horses by a strap, flat on his breast and head up against a sapling, I said: "Hello, John, that's a mighty small protection for your head." He replied: "Yes, Captain, but if there was a ground squirrel's hole near by I think I could get into it." I had it from one of our men who is good authority that a certain fellow was stretched out behind a good sized stump with his nose within twelve inches of a pile of filth, when another seeing the situation and coveting that stump for himself exclaimed, "look at that stuff near your face." "Pshaw, go away! it smells sweet as a rose," he replied, and still stuck to his stump.

After what seemed an interminable time the enemy gradually ceased the furious cannonade of that hill. One of the men looking towards the west remarked that the sun seemed to be in exactly the place it was an hour before and he believed it was "hung in the tops of them trees."

Having placed the dead on the caissons, about dark we moved back to our former place behind the ridge. After consultation with friends, it was deemed best to bury McCorkle and Fairfax near our resting place for the night. This was done with much difficulty, in the tired broken down, sleepy condition of the men. The graves were marked so that their friends easily found them shortly afterwards. If I were asked to select representatives of the two types of men composing our battery I would name Fairfax and McCorkle—the former the Cavalier element, the latter the Scotch Irish—each the perfect flower of his type.

Graham and his section rejoined us after night fall almost worn out with the hard work of the day under Pelham, but happy in the consciousness of having contributed their part of the great victory.

Next day we were posted across the railroad in a bottom, almost in line with position of the 13th. It was a quiet day, and I visited the wounded at the hospital. My horse, so badly wounded on the 13th, had to be turned out. I took possession of Lieutenant McCorkle's horse, which I afterwards bought from his father—a nice looking little sorrel mare with whitish mane and tail. My wounded horse was taken up by Private McClanahan, of Salem Battery, who to my surprise cured him up and brought him to me afterwards. I paid him for his trouble, etc., and sold the horse to Lieutenant Cole Davis.

That fight on Dead Horse Hill weighed heavily on me for sometime. I could not understand Jackson's order and our sacrifice seemed useless. Not one of the guns on my left fired a shot so far as I could learn. But Jackson ordered it and I tried to think it was all right, but never ceased to mourn the loss of those splendid officers and men.

CHAPTER 7

FAREWELL TO THE ROCKBRIDGE ARTILLERY

A MAGNIFICENT DISPLAY of the Aurora Borealis was witnessed the night of the 14th. A short time after the battle I was ordered to report to General Early in the neighborhood of Port Royal. I spent the balance of the winter on picket duty, having a comfortable camp on the Gay Mont Estate owned by a Mr. Bernard. I was only once called on for service, in an attempt to drive off gun boats at Port Royal. Our firing was not effective on account of the poor quality of the Confederate ammunition we had to use. Early and D. H. Hill were present looking on. Old D. H. expressed thorough disgust at our poor work.

I had to ride occasionally with General Early up and down the river and found him kind and considerate. Our outpost life proved more agreeable than we had expected. Our camp was among pines on the southern slope of a ridge and was thus protected in a measure from the cold north and west winds. Our larder was fairly well supplied and in February (1863) we began to get choice fish from the Rappahannock River. It was somewhat lonely, the

rest of our battalion being far back in the county, some
twenty miles, and we had few acquaintances among
Early's people.

Once Colonel Brown came to see me and after supper took me with him to call on the Gay Mont people.[1]
Here we found Pelham and we were just beginning to
have a pleasant time—there being two young ladies
among the inmates—when in steps General "Rooney"
Lee and a couple of his staff. At once it seemed as if an
iceberg had floated into the room. Such frigid dignity I
never encountered and so it was not long before Colonel
Brown, Pelham and myself took our leave, having been
completely frozen out.

Early in March (1863), we were ordered to Hamilton's Crossing into a cold unprotected camp. Here I
received official notice of my promotion to major and
assignment to a battalion of which former Captain D. G.
McIntosh was the senior major and was ordered to report
to him some miles distant in the direction of my late
winter quarters. I was not disappointed in being the junior
officer for I had heard that McIntosh was a very fine
officer and it was agreeable to me not to have the responsibility. It required several days to wind up affairs as
captain of the battery and to turn over the command to
Captain Archie Graham, my successor.

It was very gratifying to receive, as I did, many
expressions of confidence and respect from the men of the
old battery and regrets at my having to leave them. Some
I knew, would be glad to be rid of me. It was in this camp
I had to make several details of men to wash, with tobacco

---

[1]Gay Mont was a beautiful estate with a formal garden, located on the
Rappahhannock River about 20 miles below Fredericksburg, Virginia. The
antebellum life here is described in *Welcum Hinges* (E. P. Dutton & Co., N.Y.,
1942). See also James River Garden Club, *Historic Gardens of Virginia*
(Richmond, 1923), 234-238.

decoctions, horses of the battery infested with vermin. For this, two Rockbridge men, Tom Wade and Alfred Gold, never forgave me; as I learned, when canvassing for the Legislature in 1871, that it was for this reason they would not vote for me.

A prayer meeting, with my consent, was held at my quarters the night before leaving. Among the petitions were some for the divine blessing upon myself. After the meeting came heartfelt farewells and affectionate good byes. I was deeply moved by the unexpected character of my parting with the old battery and I still cherish the remembrance of it as one of the happiest hours of my life. I have more than once been told by Joe F. Shaner that that prayer meeting was the starting point in his conversion to Christ.

In a few days I reported to Major McIntosh by whom I was kindly received. He was a man of superior intellect, educated, dignified and rather reserved, but during my short stay with him my relations with him were agreeable. Here I found Hale Houston, his ordinance officer and William Houston who I think was chaplain of his battalion. William Houston did not like McIntosh and his stay with him was not of long duration. Hale, I think, was with him till the end at Appomattox and I know was highly esteemed and appreciated by McIntosh. My impression is that both declined to surrender and rode out together. It was my happy privilege to number both William and Hale Houston among my very best friends.

After about two weeks with McIntosh he sent me with Hurt's Battery—in which was the noted Whitworth Rifle—some miles down the Rappahannock, probably near Rappahannock Academy, to look after the enemy's gun boats. But there was no occasion to use our long range Whitworth as the boats did not come up to our neighborhood. We spent near a month here, and it being an early Spring I found excellent pasture near camp, to which I had the horses taken daily, with harness on, ready for emergencies. Captain Hurt saw that they were well groomed twice a day, with the result that they soon shed their winter coats and improved very rapidly, and when we rejoined the battalion just before Chancellorsville they would hardly believe they were the same animals we took away. Colonel Lindsay Walker, Chief of Artillery of the 3rd Corps—ours—was greatly surprised and delighted to see them in such good condition and complimented us, Hurt and myself, on their wonderful improvement, the teams being far ahead of any in the 3rd Corps.

In the battle of Chancellorsville (May 1-6, 1863) I had very little to do. The battalion following along in rear of Jackson's lines as they routed and pursued the fleeing enemy. At dark we pulled out into a field just in rear of our line of battle, where we rested for the night but got little sleep on account of the occasional but most terrific outbreaks in our immediate front, and constant cries for water and calls for help by the enemy's wounded among whom we bivouacked. We gave them all the help and succor we could and were amply repaid by their heartfelt thanks.

Early next morning McIntosh pulled out into the road and started to the front, but soon halted behind other batteries standing in column. Other batteries crowded up behind ours. Here we waited some time when "Jeb" Stuart came dashing along (he had been put in command of Jackson's forces after the latter was stricken) asking in a quick, impatient manner: "Whose artillery is this? What are your orders?" The reply: "McIntosh's Battalion, no orders except to move to front in rear of battalion in front." His only reply or rather exclamation was: "O for a general of artillery" and away he galloped to the front. By the way, he was riding "Josh," your uncle Jim's superb five year old bay, my brother Jim being a courier of Stuart's. It was not long before the front battalion—Pegram's—turned square to right followed by McIntosh and proceeding some four or five hundred yards wheeled into battery and at once went to work on the enemy's artillery at the Chancellor house. Pegram and McIntosh outnumbered them and soon stopped them and drove them from the field; some of their guns were left standing unlimbered.

In the meantime the Chancellor house was set on fire by our shells, not intentionally, but unavoidably as the enemy's guns were all about the old mansion and out-houses. At this juncture a column of infantry approached the house off on our right, and nobody could make out to which army it belonged even with the best glasses. So, Pegram and I agreed to gallop over there and find out, and to our joy they turned out to be Confederates. The house was in full blaze, muskets constantly going off inside, but not a living being in sight. General Hooker, a short while before had been pretty badly shocked by one of our shells shattering a pillar against which he was leaning. Soon Pegram and McIntosh were over there and the enemy, having retreated to a strong line of breast works in rear of the dense black jack forest, they shelled them for sometime, drawing the enemy's artillery fire, but they overshot us and did little damage.

About this time General Lee rode up with some of his staff from the direction of Salem Church followed by Confederate infantry. Cheering broke out and was taken up by the various bodies of Confederate troops as they converged at this central point. We were not disturbed by the enemy and the remainder of the day was spent in happy congratulations upon the victory, enquiring for personal friends, and looking over the field where Jackson's old division fought. The loss to our county and our Southland was beyond estimate in the fall of Jackson alone. Next was the death of General Frank Paxton at the head of the Stonewall Brigade—in my judgment the best specimen of a Scotch-Irish soldier given by Rockbridge to our cause.

Then came Captain Greenlee Davidson of the Letcher Artillery, who mortally wounded, was being lifted into an ambulance as our battalion went into the fight— one of the three brothers who yielded up their young lives in defense of the South. A half-brother of your Grandmother Poague, John Henry Paxton, fell on another part of this extended battle field near Fredericksburg. The blood of these three soldiers was of the same strain as that flowing in your veins. Other Rockbridge men were slain at Chancellorsville making it an occasion of mourning as well as rejoicing to many of us. A short while before this battle while visiting in the old Stonewall Brigade I called at General Paxton's quarters and had a pleasant talk with him. While speculating on the personal hazards of the approaching campaign he remarked: "Ah, Poague, if the rest of us poor sinners had "Old Jack's" religion and assurance of faith, with what little thought of personal safety we would go into battle." It is known now that he had settled that great question by a confession of Christ.

In this battle on the right of the plank road in the woods nearest Chancellorsville, the slaughter on both sides was as great as I ever saw on any field, except, perhaps, that of the enemy in front of the railroad cut at 2nd Manassas.

A friend in the College Company told me that in the charge they marched over a line of North Carolinians lying on their faces, stamping them as they passed, when one fellow exclaimed: "that's all right, we don't mind it, go ahead boys."

Sometime after this, while camped near Hamilton's Crossing, I was sent for by General Lindsay Walker, 3rd Corps Chief of Artillery, who informed me he was about forming a new battalion and that I was to be placed in command of it. This was a genuine surprise, and highly gratifying, as I was a newcomer in the 3rd Corps and a comparative stranger. I attribute my selection mainly to my success in getting into good shape the teams of Hurt's Battery while on picket down the Rappahannock. So you see my training on the farm where I had learned about the care and handling of horses, stood me in good stead.

This kind of knowledge was of great importance to artillery officers. There came a time afterwards when some batteries and even battalions became sadly inefficient because of poor teams. On the terrible retreat from Petersburg when, at Amelia Court House, General Lee was arranging his forces for the final death grapple with the overpowering forces of Grant, two battalions of artillery were selected from the large number at hand, to accompany his infantry and be interposed between the enemy and his artillery, ordnance, commissary and quartermaster trains moving on interior roads and these select battalions were Colonels McIntosh's and Poague's. This I have always esteemed the highest honor ever bestowed on my command. This distinction was due in large measure to the superior condition of our teams.

But to go back. Before leaving the vicinity of Fred-

ericksburg for the Valley and Pennsylvania three batteries
reported to me, *viz:* Captain A. W. Utterback's—formerly
Brooke's of Fauquier and Madison Counties, Virginia;
Captain James Wyatt's—from Albemarle County, Virginia; and Captain George Ward's from Canton, Mississippi. The first and second had seen some service with the
Army of Northern Virginia. The third had not been in
Virginia long. Soon after they reported, we started on
the march for the Valley and a Battalion organization
was effected on this march: Dr. R. L. Hoard, of Albemarle, reporting to me as surgeon; Captain T. T. Hill,
nephew of General A. P. Hill, as ordnance officer; and
J. D. Tulloss, of Utterback's battery, was appointed by
me quartermaster and commissary and was commissioned
captain. These turned out to be good officers, being active
and industrious in fitting up and equipping their depart-
ments. Their work was done under difficulties as we
were constantly on the march.

On going into camp near Berryville, Virginia, Captain Joseph Graham, commanding a North Carolina
battery, reported to me, under rather amusing circumstances. I was lying sprawled on the grass in my shirt
sleeves when a splendidly uniformed officer rode up
mounted on a magnificent dark bay stallion followed by
a mounted orderly. The officer asked me if I could tell
him where he would find Major Poague, the commander
of the battalion. On replying that I supposed I was the
man he was looking for he was evidently much surprised.
After a moment's hesitation and with something of an
incredulous stare and a smile, he said, "Well, if you are
the commander of Poague's Battalion, I have been ordered
to report for assignment to your command." I replied:
"All right, Captain, glad to have you with us. Won't you
dismount and rest a little in the shade." "Thank you, no,"

he responded, "I must see about getting my battery in camp."

Calling his Irish orderly, he directed him to dismount and hand me a paper he gave him. Rising to a sitting position and glancing over his orders I told him where to park his guns and that he would receive the usual orders for the march next day. With a salute he wheeled and rode off much disappointed, I was sure, in the appearance of his commander. And I guess he had a right to be, for my coat was doubled up under my head thereby concealing the collar with the star and only a field glass lying near to indicate that the dusty, unkempt, common-looking individual he addressed might be an officer. The Irishman was simply disgusted, as his features plainly showed, and I have no doubt, he so expressed himself to his comrades.

No officer, especially one in command, ought to allow carelessness or indifference as to his appearance. General Lee put on his best uniform to meet Grant, and the latter apologized for being found in a soiled fatigue suit. It was hard to rid myself of the impression my first interview with Ashby produced, when I found him with nothing but a red flannel shirt on.

GETTYSBURG

WE NEXT CROSSED THE POTOMAC and in a few days were at Gettysburg (July 1-3, 1863). Somewhere on this march I had received orders to report to General J. J. Pettigrew, move and camp with him and to receive my orders from and through him. He had the largest, best equipped, finest looking brigade of the whole army, and was himself a fine officer, polished gentleman and always handsomely dressed. After the fight opened the first day, he moved his brigade to the front, directing me to remain where we were, near Cashtown, and await orders. The two battalions, Pegram's and McIntosh's being ahead of me were ordered up and put into the fight.

After hours of waiting I was ordered up and posted on the right of the road in a fairly good position but the battle was about over, the enemy having been driven back to Cemetery Hill. Next morning I was placed a little further to the right and further to front by General W. N. Pendleton, and was directed by him to look over and examine all the country to my right so as to be able to post my batteries in the most eligible positions in case I should be sent in that direction.

About 9 A.M. while reconnoitering that region southwest of Big Round Top I ran across General Lee with two or three couriers, riding through the woods. He called me to him and asked, "Have you seen General Longstreet or any of his troops anywhere in this neighborhood." I answered that I had not. Then getting a glimpse of a small body of men on foot moving along the edge of the woods he dispatched one of his couriers to learn who they were. He then asked me how far I had been towards the mountain, pointing towards Round Top, and my object in being out there, etc., and then as soon as the courier returned he asked, "Are they Longstreet's men?" The answer was, "They are not, but a small detachment returning to their command in the direction of Gettysburg." Then showing disappointment and impatience by his manner and tone he said, "I wonder where General Longstreet can be."

I was impressed with the idea that General Lee was much worried about something and not long after I fell in with General Lindsay Walker and told him of my interview with General Lee and we concluded that the general was disappointed in not finding General Longstreet where he expected him to be. This incident tends to confirm the belief—well nigh universal among Confederates—that Longstreet was responsible for the loss of the battle. An article by the eminent military critic, Colonel Henderson, an Englishman and biographer of Stonewall Jackson, makes it clear beyond doubt that the indictment of Longstreet by his old comrades for our failure at Gettysburg is true.[1]

---

[1] Some recent studies have taken a much more favorable view of Longstreet's conduct at Gettysburg. See Donald B. Sanger and Thomas R. Hay, *James*

About 1 P.M. some officers of my battalion called my attention to the movement of a column far off to our right—perhaps three to four miles—but no one could tell who they were or even in what direction it was moving, simply the glistening of gun barrels over a dark mass for a distance of apparently two or three hundred yards. I at once sent an officer to report the fact to General Lee, who was not far from my position. I was at once sent for and questioned in a way I can never forget.

"Major," he said, "you have sent some rather vague information about a body of troops somewhere. Please tell me all you know about it." (Note the Q (question) and A (answer) form of the following.):

A. "All I know is that a column of infantry, as well as I could make out, is in motion far to our right." Q. "What troops are they, the enemy's or ours?" A. "I don't know; it was impossible to tell."

Q. "In what direction are they moving?" A. "I couldn't tell; their course is directly to or from us."

Q. "On what road are they?" A. "That I don't know."

Q. "Well, Major, what *do* you know?" A. "Only what I reported."

He then said, "It is very important while in enemy's country that officers obtain all the information possible about the geography of the region and especially about the different roads. This can be gotten by inquiring of the citizens of the neighborhood. Their reports should be as full and definite as can be made."

All this was intended as a reproof. Although I felt conscious of no failure of duty under the circumstances;

Longstreet (Baton Rouge, 1952), 156-188; and Kenneth P. Williams, *Lincoln Finds a General* (New York, 1949—), II, 724-729.

still at the time, I was mortified. Indeed, I felt something like I did when as a boy of twelve or fourteen, I used to flunk on the Shorter Catechism under the questioning of good old Parson Ewing—somewhat sheepish and in a bad humor.

Longstreet, who should have attacked *early in the morning,* did not begin the fight until about 4 P.M. We had nothing to do but look on, and so up to end of the second day my battalion had not fired a shot, though ready and expecting to be called on at any minute.

Next morning I secured good positions for my batteries, that is for ten (10) guns—rifles and Napoleons. Wyatt and Graham were posted on the extreme right of Hill's Corps with a small body of woods on their right and on a line with the end of the woods. Further still to the right Utterback and Ward were stationed just on the other side of the wood and about four hundred yards from the other two batteries. The position of Utterback and Ward was the best, I think, on the whole of the line, just in front of the point of Pickett's attacks and afforded a fine view of the whole stretch of open country from Little Round Top on my right nearly to Gettysburg College at my left, the very best position to witness the attack on the third day by Longstreet's left and Hill's right, being at the junction of the two wings.

General Lee often stopped here. About 10 A.M. he was here viewing the field, when a handsomely equipped officer came cantering from the right about 75 yards in front of our lines and when he got opposite our guns, General Lee called out to him, "My friend! this way if you please," and beckoning him to come to where he was—at my guns. The officer wheeled and trotted up saluting as he halted in front of the general, who exclaimed with affected surprise, "Ah! Major, excuse me;

I thought you might be some countryman who had missed his way. Let me say to you and to these young officers, that I am an old reconnoitering officer and have always found it best to go afoot, *and not expose oneself needlessly.*"

Dearing at once caught his meaning and saluting, with some embarrassment passed through the guns and rode off in rear of the lines. While awaiting the signal for the artillery to open, I went back for a chat with two or three infantry officers just in my rear and at the left of their regiment which was lying prone upon the ground. They were speculating as to the chances of getting safely through the impending fight. All were hopeful, but I learned afterwards that they all fell in the charge. Col. Stuart, a very handsome man and commanding the Regiment, 56th Virginia, I think, being mortally wounded. His regiment was the left of Kemper's Brigade, and passed through our guns in the charge.

My orders were to open on the enemy's position in front at the signal—2 cannon shots to my right in quick succession—and that as soon as our infantry, in the charge to follow, reached the crest, to proceed as rapidly as possible to the summit with all my guns, and there be governed by circumstances. Not a word was said about following the infantry as they advanced to the attack.

We kept up a deliberate cannonade until Pickett's men passed to the front. (Then I ordered up the 6 howitzers, which had been stationed in a somewhat protected locality at the lower end of wood). I watched with intense interest and anxiety the advance of the infantry on both sides of me. When about two-thirds of the way to the crest, there was confusion and giving away in Hill's troops, most of them turning back, though some went on apparently to within a very short distance of the enemy's lines.

As soon as Pickett's men reached the crest I gave the order to limber to the front—that meant to prepare to advance. But before starting I began to be perplexed and disturbed by seeing small bodies of men coming back and the number increasing every moment until the awful truth began to force itself upon me that the attack had failed.

At this very critical moment General Pickett himself appeared on the line of my guns on horseback and near one of them looking intently to the front. Nobody was with him. Though not acquainted with him, I knew who he was, and at once rode to him and said after saluting, "General, my orders are that as soon as our troops get the hill I am to move as rapidly as possible to their support. But I don't like the look of things up there." He made no reply and didn't even turn his head to see who I was, but continued to gaze with an expression on his face of sadness and pain.

At that instant a Virginia flag was borne rapidly along and in rear of the stone wall by a horseman, and again I said, "General, is that Virginia flag carried by one of our men or by the enemy." No reply. I then said, "What do you think I ought to do under the circumstances. Our men are leaving the hill." "I think you had better save your guns," was his answer, and at once rode off. I did not know exactly what he meant. But by this time I knew what I ought to do, and at once prepared to meet any advance of the enemy by ordering up the six howitzers which had been stationed in a somewhat protected spot at the lower end of the woods.

Scarcely had General Pickett gotten away, when General Lee came up, calling me to him. His first question

was, "How are you off for ammunition, Major." I told
him about how much we had left—probably one fourth—
but that I would soon have up six howitzers with full
chests. "Ah! that's well; we may need them," he said,
evidently pleased as he saw us getting ready to receive
the enemy in case of an advance. The general spent some
time with us surveying the field and then as the little
parties of those from that encircling tempest of death on
the crest, began to arrive, he would address to them some
kindly words, saying to nearly all, "Men, go to the brook
down there," pointing to the lower end of the woods,
"and rest and refresh yourselves." He was perfectly calm
and self-possessed, with no trace of the impatience and
worry I had observed in my two previous interviews.

As to General Pickett's conduct and his exact whereabouts during the fight much of criticism has been spoken
and written, and much also in his defense.[2] I myself saw
him but once, and then at the precise time and place
above mentioned. My new command acquitted itself most
creditably and won my admiration by their cool and
deliberate behaviour under the hot fire. My little sorrel
mare was horribly mutilated by a shell almost severing
her hind quarters, having curved over her head cutting
in twain and scattering my saddle and overcoat tied
behind. Fortunately I had just dismounted to see after
one of the guns. The saddle was a genuine McClellan
picked up on field of Port Republic, and appropriated
with the approval of General Winder. My overcoat was
one that had been made in Lexington for General Jackson,
but being rather small for him, I bought it. It was of the
best material and the best one I owned during the war.

I was at Gettysburg in 1889 along with the survivors

2See Monroe F. Cockrell, "Where Was Pickett at Gettysburg?", an
unpublished study, copies of which have been deposited in various libraries,
including that of Emory University.

of Pickett's Division. While at the place occupied by Utterback's and Ward's guns and pointing out their position to Colonel Batchelder, the Federal officer whose duty it was to locate and mark the positions of Confederate troops, one of Pickett's men who was standing near us, asked if I was the officer in command of the artillery at that place on the 3rd of July, 1863. On telling him I was, he exclaimed, "Well, I declare! I was certain I saw you and your horse torn to pieces by a shell. I reckon I have told it a hundred times and would have been willing to swear to it! Well, colonel, I am so delighted to see you, I feel like I must give you a good hug." And with that he gave me a most cordial embrace.

The Philadelphia Brigade, the host of Pickett's people on this occasion, had a tent near the noted clump of trees on the once bloody crest, and in it a number of casks of lager beer placed on and surmounted by blocks of ice for the refreshment of their guests, while I and a friend were sipping our beer (it was a very hot day) an old Confederate, after draining his tin cup remarked to the Federals, "If you all had had this up here that hot day in July, 1863, we would have stayed here."

General Lee got away from Gettysburg without difficulty and offered battle to Meade for several days near Hagerstown and then recrossed the Potomac on pontoons he had built while confronting his adversary. My battalion was the last artillery to cross, followed by Pettigrew's Brigade—the rear guard. As his brigade was waiting for everything to get across a small body of Federal cavalry made a dash at the rear guard but were quickly repulsed. In this affair General Pettigrew was slain, to the great grief of the whole army.

CHAPTER 9

RELAXATION AND PROMOTION

WE SPENT SOMETIME in the Valley, and then moved leisurely across the Blue Ridge to the neighborhood of Culpeper Court House and finally encamped near Orange Court House and spent the time mostly in drilling and fitting out the batteries with some good rifles and Napoleons, in place of the short range howitzers. I was much troubled that summer and fall with chills and fever, which interfered with full enjoyment of the long season of rest and the opportunities for social enjoyment within reach of us in a most hospitable and cultivated community.

While at Hagerstown, I bought from the quartermaster department, or rather accepted in payment for my little mare killed at Gettysburg, a large fine looking bay mare impressed in Pennsylvania and paid for by our quartermaster in Confederate money. But as she was too heavy for the saddle I exchanged her for one bought by my father in Rockbridge named Julia. This horse lasted me through the war, although frequently under hot fire. At first she was gentle enough, but after being stung by gravels once or twice hurled by shots striking near her, she finally got to be almost unmanageable in battle and gave me much trouble. After the war I gave her to your Grandma Poague for a buggy nag, but she never got used to the sound of a gun. Barclay and Bess may remember her.

In the fall of 1863 (October) came the Bristoe campaign in which Gen. Lee flanked Meade's Army. Our corps—A. P. Hill's—was in the lead and my battalion near the front. About 1 P.M. we came upon a division of the enemy cooking dinner in a bottom beyond a small stream, all unconscious of our approach. My battalion was ordered up and at once opened on them. They were at once scattered and such scampering and skedaddling was hardly ever seen. On our right was a strong force of infantry moving along the railroad. General Hill wheeled several brigades into line and attacked them, but they did not run as the others had, but dropping down behind the embankment, received our troops with such a murderous fire, that after losing a large number our attacking force was driven back in some confusion. The enemy didn't follow.

Hill then placed two of his artillery battalions, McIntosh's and mine, on a little ridge overlooking the railroad and tried to shell them out of cover, but they didn't budge. On the contrary McIntosh was charged and some of his guns captured, but were held only a short time, their captors being driven back and the guns recovered by one of Hill's brigades. The enemy soon moved on and got away with comparatively small loss.

About this time General Lee came on the field, and had an interview with General Hill who explained the failure and proposed to push on in pursuit. One who was near enough to hear what passed told me that General

Lee's reply was "General Hill, I think you had better attend to the burying of your dead," and that he was evidently not pleased with Hill's management of the affair. After the fight was over our men got to chasing and catching rabbits of which there were great numbers all about us. Burying comrades and running rabbits at the same time! Such is war!

We didn't advance any further, but went back to our former camps where we rested in peace and quiet until General Meade advanced and crossed the Rapidan. General Lee promptly met him and for several days offered battle, but Meade suddenly by night stole back across the river. It is now known, from a published letter of General Lee, that he had made a disposition of his forces to attack General Meade the morning after his withdrawal.

While in line of battle at this place—Mine Run—an old friend from St. Joe, Missouri, William Ritchie, stumbled on me as I was preparing my dinner of coffee, bread, and beef hash. Recognition was instant and mutual and as he shared my luncheon, he told me he was looking for General Lee, to offer his services either as a scout or spy, that he had served on the frontier in Missouri as a spy, was captured, tried by drumhead court martial and sentenced to be executed next morning. That night he made his escape, left that part of the country for the East, to undertake the same kind of service with General Lee. He was a typical frontiersman of those stirring days in Missouri and Kansas, fearless, shrewd, active, and ready for any desperate enterprise against his mortal enemies, the Kansas Jayhawkers. I directed him to General Lee's temporary quarters. With a hearty shake of the hand I bade him good-bye, wishing him godspeed in his dangerous vocation. I never laid eyes on nor heard of him again.

While lying here in line of battle, I saw a good deal of General Lee and other officers, and was much impressed with their eagerness for a fight. When I asked General A. P. Hill what he thought the enemy would do, he said: "I don't know, but I wish they would show their hand, and give us a chance at them." I thought he was hoping to get even with them on the Bristoe affair. General Lee looked more martial and imposing than ever I saw him. As for his subordinates in the lower grades, they were not spoiling for a fight and were not sorry to hear that Meade had recrossed the river, and some of us with much satisfaction went back to the comfortable quarters we had left in a grove of magnificent oak and hickory trees on the farm of Mr. Nalle, who was not made unhappy by our presence. We had somehow gotten the idea that we were to winter here and made ourselves as comfortable as possible, having chimneys built to our tents and other conveniences provided. Here our courts martial got to work, and many unfortunates suffered novel and amusing penalties for petty misdeeds.

But not for long were we to enjoy this comfortable and attractive place, for I received orders to proceed to Lindsay's Turnout[1] on Central Railroad, some miles west of Gordonsville, and place the battalions in winter quarters. Here were found water and an abundance of timber near the station. Huts and stables were soon built and also a log church and the men passed the winter in tolerable comfort.

Our Presbyterian chaplain, Reverend James M. Wharey, had services on Sundays and prayer meeting once during the week. Reverend Hugh Scott, of the Epis-

---

[1]Lindsay's Turnout was about three and one-half miles southwest of Gordonsville, where the highway crosses the railroad. See *Atlas to Accompany the War of the Rebellion: Official Records of the Union and Confederate Armies* (Washington, 1891-1895), Plate 100.

copal Church, visited camp preaching a number of times
and holding communion. All of us except some of the
Baptist attended the communion services. We had a visit
and preaching also by Dr. J. B. Jeter, a noted Baptist minister from Richmond. A large number of the men were
professing Christians; many of them highly intelligent
and educated gentlemen; and not a few earnest and
devoted followers of Christ.

This was my only quiet winter of the war—no
alarms, not a gun fired, not a sound of war, so different
from my experience the two preceding winters and the
one that was to follow. To myself, however, it was the
most trying and least pleasant of all, on account of my
duties as president of a court martial for the artillery of
the 3rd Corps, all of which was in winter quarters in the
neighborhood of Gordonsville. Most of the cases were for
minor offences, but a number were tried for desertion,
and some were condemned to die. The day for the execu-
tion of one of these arrived and the stake or post to which
he was to be bound was set, when a pardon from
Richmond saved him. For a brief space there was rejoicing among the members of the court, but this was soon
hushed by the dismal grind of that awful mill—military
necessity—and when the distressing business was finally
ended by an order for the discharge of the court it was
as the lifting of a great burden from our hearts.

While in winter quarters here, I was promoted to
lieutenant colonel and Captain George Ward, of the
Mississippi battery, was made major and assigned to duty
with me. Ward was a most efficient officer and a perfect
gentleman and above all a most consistent Christian. Our
intercourse was most pleasant; to me, he was a delightful
companion and I became warmly attached to him.

An incident occurred at this camp that gave some of

us much amusement but it was at the expense of our
worthy chaplain. When Dr. Jeter visited us, he stopped
with Captain Utterback, a thorough-going Baptist. A day
or two after his arrival Reverend Wharey called on him
after breakfast and invited him and Captain Utterback
to dine with us at 3 P.M. I knew nothing of it, and so
had my frugal meal of corn bread and bacon all to myself,
as Mr. Wharey had not returned. Before our cook, Joe,
had cleared away the crusts, in steps Captain Utterback
and Dr. Jeter. After sitting a while and chatting pleasantly
they took their leave.

On Wharey's return about sunset I told him what he
had missed. He instantly threw up both hands exclaiming:
"Well, I do declare! Don't you know I invited them to
dinner and rode over to Mr. Cowherds and forgot all
about it! It is too bad. What am I to do about it?"

"Go to Utterback and apologize and explain if you
can," I said.

"I must make amends somehow," he added. "Can't
we have them to breakfast. I'll go right now and ask
them." And so he did.

Our larder at this time was in a state of depletion
and it was no easy matter to get up a decent camp breakfast. Joe was loaded with Confederate "shin plasters" and
started out with orders not to return without a supply of
eatables. After ransacking the neighborhood he came back
with a very scanty supply of things for breakfast, among
them an old hen. He went around camp and borrowed a
little butter, just enough for one meal. We happened to
have some genuine coffee and a good supply of sorghum
molasses. Thus, by exhausting our resources, we managed
to have a fairly good breakfast, which was to be at 8:30.

Next morning as things were being prepared, it
began to rain and in five minutes it was pouring down

and continued to do so until Joe informed us that breakfast had been ready an hour and wouldn't keep any
longer. Nothing was heard from our expected guests and
there being no prospect of the rain holding up, it was
decided after consultation that the best thing to do was
to eat breakfast. We decided that we should utilize the
situation to pay off a debt of courtesy by asking our
neighboring mess, the adjutant and surgeon to join us,
which they were prompt to do, and all hands enjoyed the
spread, not knowing when we would get another decent
meal.

Brother Wharey's spirits were much revived as he
congratulated himself on having extricated himself in a
measure from the mortifying fix he had gotten himself
in the day before. About the time we finished breakfast,
the rain also got through with its work and suddenly
stopped. As I was having my horse saddled to go to the
session of the court martial in came a messenger from
Captain Utterback saying that he and Dr. Jeter were prevented by the rain from coming to breakfast but that they
would come up and take dinner with us. This capped the
climax of Brother Wharey's misfortunes. Nearly everything went into that breakfast, and now both he and Joe
were in despair.

I had to go off to the court and didn't return until
about 4:00 P.M. and as I dismounted I heard Wharey
calling out in a heartbroken tone: "Joe! Joe! Come on
Joe!" But poor Joe couldn't get the fritters to do right
"case he didn't have no grease hardly to brown 'em
with." Fritters and sorghum was the desert they had
decided on, but Brother Wharey told me that the whole
thing was a dismal failure, and he was never so much
mortified in his life. But I am sure Dr. Jeter had a lot of
fun out of our effort to entertain. The first time he called

I noticed a merry twinkle about his eye as occasionally he glanced at the crusts on the improvised table. Captain Utterback and I had many an uproarious laugh at Brother Wharey but it was found to have left a very sore spot and fifteen years after the war he told me he had not gotten over it.

In high contrast with this entertainment shortly afterwards was a dining at the home of Honorable William C. Rives which I attended in company with Lieutenant Rives, his nephew, and some half dozen other officers of the battalion.[2] A most sumptuous and elegant repast it was. We enjoyed the good things to eat, but I, at least, was somewhat ill at ease on account of the dignity and stateliness of the affair. Both the host and the hostess were very kind and gracious and were most entertaining in conversation. Mrs. Rives was rather severe on Lincoln as a "prince from the lowest of the people," referring to that period in Jewish history when the Lord punished them for wrongdoing when he permitted princes of the lowest of the people to rule over them.

As the spring opened up there were signs on all sides of preparation for the great campaign of 1864. Furloughs ceased, men were called in from various details; and inspection, reviews, etc., became the order of the day. The review of Longstreet's Corps on its arrival from his Tennessee campaigns was, even at that late period of the war, as imposing and inspiring as any I had before witnessed. No one thought it would be the last. All were hopeful and confident as to the issue of the gigantic struggle with Grant and his immense host, notwithstand-

---

[2]William Cabell Rives (1793-1868) was at this time a member of the Confederate Congress. Before the war he served in the U. S. House of Representatives and Senate and was twice Minister to France. The Rives home was "Castle Hill," a beautiful place with formal garden, between Gordonsville and Charlottesville.

ing we all knew that General Lee was at a great disadvantage in numbers, equipment and in food supplies
for man and beast. Yet such was our faith in our commander, that we went into the contest cheerfully and not
without some curiosity as to Grant's plan of campaign.
You football boys, as you have trotted out on the field
against an admittedly stronger team, can form some
conception of the intense interest that filled the breasts of
Lee's men as they marched in the direction of the
Wilderness.

CHAPTER 10

A SEASON OF SLAUGHTER: WILDERNESS
THROUGH COLD HARBOR

WE BROKE UP WINTER QUARTERS—not before the 29th of April—our movements depending on those of the enemy. My battalion took position so as to command the approaches to the bridge over the Rapidan near Liberty Mills. On May 4th we moved with Wilcox's Division along the turnpike towards Chancellorsville and bivouacked that night near Verdiersville. As we moved on next morning with Wilcox, about 9:00 A.M., under orders from General A. P. Hill to send a battery to the front to report to General Heth, I went forward with Richard's (formerly Ward's) Battery and moved with the advance guard striking the enemy's cavalry about 10:00 A.M. Skirmishing became lively at once. Unusually large numbers of enemy were killed as we pressed them back vigorously. Our advance did not halt until we ran up against a heavy force posted in the Wilderness (May 5-7, 1864) about two miles below Parker's Store.

There was no room for more than one gun in the road, yet General Heth kept all four of the guns in column right up at the front, until I prevailed on him to let me send three of them back. This is but one of the many examples of infantry officers' manner of handling artillery.

It was not long before the enemy made a heavy attack, forced our line back at first and got our gun. Lieutenant George fought his gun until run over by infantry on both sides of the road. He and a number of his men and horses were wounded. The enemy did not get our gun away and the terrific struggle continued with varying fortune until dark. A lieutenant and some men of the 44th North Carolina seized the piece—a beautiful 3-inch rifle—and ran it back within our main line.

In the meantime the rest of the battalion was thrown into battery about five hundred yards back in a little clearing on the left of the turnpike. This was the only place available for artillery and my guns took up the entire space. I posted the guns about midway of the field which left an open area about 300 yards long to our front. Here we spent the night. Heth's and Wilcox's men had barely held their own in the fight, losing quite heavily.

At early dawn, learning that the captured gun was within our lines, I went with a detachment and had it brought by hand and placed in position with the other guns. As I went along the Plank Road to get the gun I was surprised to see the unusual condition of things. Nearly all the men were still asleep. One long row of muskets was stacked in the road. Another row made an acute angle with the road and still another was almost at right angles, and here and there could be seen bunches of stacked guns.

I asked an officer the meaning of the apparent confusion and unreadiness of our lines and was told that Hill's men had been informed that they were to be relieved by fresh troops before daylight, and were expecting the relieving forces every minute. I asked where the Yankees were. He didn't know certainly, but supposed they were in the woods in front. He struck me as being very indifferent and not at all concerned about the situation. I could not help feeling troubled, although I supposed somebody knew about how things were.

Just after I had gotten back to the battalion and placed the recaptured gun in position, pop! pop! began the skirmishers and soon a terrific outbreak of musketry showed that the enemy were attacking in force. For I knew that our troops could hardly be making the attack, with our lines situated as I had found them to be. For a long time the firing seemed to be stationary and then gradually it began to draw nearer. Soon our men were seen to be falling back slowly on the right of the road, through a thick growth of blackjack. None of our wounded retired by the road but kept in the dense woods. I could yet do nothing to help our sorely pressed men because the firing indicated that the combatants were very close together and all across the road from our position.

Closer and closer the uproar came and at last the enemy's skirmishers appeared at the edge of the thicket in our front and opened fire on us. I had directed our men to pile up rails, logs, etc., at each gun for protection from bullets that now came constantly our way. Knowing that the skirmishers in our front meant a line of battle behind them, I ordered a slow fire to the front with short range shells. To our surprise no force showed itself, for I surely expected our guns would be charged. I had one gun in the road under Lieutenant Alexander, of the North Carolina battery, which was used with effect in causing the approaching hostiles to leave the road for the brush.

Still our troops were being pressed back until they were nearly on our flank. Several pieces on the right of the battery were turned to fire obliquely across the road on their advancing lines as indicated by the firing, for not a man could be seen in the tangle of the Wilderness.

The progress of the enemy was slow because of the stubborn resistance of Hill's men. As the latter got opposite our flank more of our guns were turned on them (the enemy) and it was our belief that this flank fire checked their advance, when they had reached a point about opposite our position.

At this critical juncture Gregg's Texans came in line of battle at a swinging gait from the rear of our position. They passed through our guns, their right near the road. General Lee was riding close behind them. Of course our firing to the front had to cease now and only two pieces continued across the road. Soon the Texans began to call to General Lee to go back, and as he seemed not to heed they became clamorous, insisting that if he did not go back they would not go forward. Several members of his staff were riding behind the general and finally one of them moved to his side and touching him on the arm said something which I could not hear. Then, turning Traveller about, he rode quietly to the rear of our line of guns, amid the cheers of the artillerymen.

This was the first time General Lee ever advanced in a charge with his troops and his action shows how critical the condition was at that juncture. I have often been asked about the appearance of General Lee at the time. He was perfectly composed, but his face expressed a kind of grim determination I had not observed either at Sharpsburg or Gettysburg. Traveller was quiet but evidently interested in the situation, as indicated by his raised head with ears pointing to the front. But there was no rearing or plunging on the part of the horse and no waving of sword by General Lee as is represented in a painting of the scene I saw some years ago. I suppose the scene was very similar to that of May 12th near the Bloody Angle.

The advance of the enemy was soon stopped by Longstreet's forces, and in fact was forced back some distance into the Wilderness on both sides of the turnpike. The Texas Brigade swept away the force in front of my guns, though suffering a great loss.

I have not been able to find any reports of General Hill's or his subordinate officers of this terrible struggle in the Wilderness. I will not undertake to say where the responsibility rests for Hill's Corps not being relieved before daylight on the 6th. A serious blunder or failure of duty in allowing daylight of the 6th to break on Hill's unprepared condition to receive the terrific attack made on his corps, rests upon somebody. We all understood that Longstreet was directed to take Hill's place by dawn, and that, as before, at Gettysburg, he failed to get there in time.

On the night of May 6th my battalion relieved by that of Colonel Richardson, moved a short distance to the rear of our lines. No fighting occurred on the 7th and on the 8th the battalion marched towards Spottsylvania Court House (May 8-21, 1864). We bivouacked that night at a place called Shady Grove and on the 9th at 10:00 A.M. went into position about 400 yards in front of the Court House on the left of the road to Fredericksburg, occupying some earthworks already commenced, and throwing up others. This was our *first experience* in an entrenched position. The position was admirable for artillery, slightly elevated with open ground, in front and on right. The woods a short distance on our left and some distance to left front were occupied by Early's infantry.

Williams' Battery on left, Wyatt next, next Utterback, with Richards on the right, was the order of formation.

From the 9th to the 21st we held this position, now and then engaging enemy's batteries, but without any serious loss or damage. Captain "Liv" (J. L.) Massie, an old college classmate and former member of the Rockbridge Artillery, was on my immediate left with his battery, and many a pleasant hour we spent together.[1] Then, too, the Rockbridge Artillery part of the time occupied a position a little to rear of our left and facing to the left ready with other guns, including one of my batteries, to meet the threatening force that had broken through at Bloody Angle on the 12th. This and Cumberland Church, April, 1865, were the only occasions I was near the old battery in line of battle, and it made me feel good to be near them.

At 3:00 P.M. on May 12th, Burnside's Corps, from a thick pine forest 200 yards in front of the salient on my left, assaulted that point. This gave us a fine opportunity, and along with Massie's guns and some of Pegram's batteries on my right assailing the dense lines of blue on the flank and our infantry at the salient pouring in a hot fire in front and at short range, Burnside was easily repulsed with heavy loss. The Confederates sustained but little damage. I suppose Grant hoped to repeat the successful action of the early morning and but for our artillery it is probable that they would have overwhelmed our line as his troops were massed under cover of the pines within a very short distance of Early's line.

In this affair one of the enemy was hurled into the air some 15 or 20 feet. General Early told me years after the war that he witnessed the remarkable occurrence.

---

[1] J. L. Massie commanded the Fluvanna Battery. He was mortally wounded, September 26, 1864, as Early fell back from Fisher's Hill. Wise, *Long Arm of Lee*, II, 889.

On May 15th the enemy's batteries opened suddenly and furiously on my position while General Lee, on foot, was examining their positions in front, as if they had discovered his presence. And perhaps with a powerful glass they had seen a prominent officer inspecting their lines. A great strapping fellow of ours actually almost dragged General Lee down into a gunpit, so anxious was he for the safety of our beloved commander.

Our surgeon, Dr. Cox, had a capacious bomb proof dug about 100 yards in rear of our position, where he could attend to the wounded "without being molested" as he put it. One day the rain came down in torrents. It had been remarked that the doctor was never seen outside of his cave and some of the men bet that it would not be long now before he would appear, or else be drowned. Not seeing anything of him a man was sent to investigate and found the place flooded and Cox hanging to the timbers overhead trying to keep his body out of the water. When asked why he didn't get out of such a place, he said: "It was getting somewhat damp, but better to endure it than expose oneself needlessly."

The day we reached this position, I learned that in the cavalry fight that preceded our arrival, Company "C", 1st Virginia—brother Jim's company—had suffered some casualties. On inquiring at the Court House, where the wounded were left, I learned that two of my personal friends had been badly wounded, Douglass McCorkle and Wilson Poague, and had just been sent away. Both reached their homes. McCorkle recovered, but Wilson died. The latter was a number one soldier and the best Christian I ever knew.

After occupying this one position for twelve days— a most admirable place for artillery—the battalion on the evening of the 21st followed Heth's Division towards

Hanover Junction. We marched all night and halted a little before daybreak to feed. At 4:00 P.M. on the 22nd we reached Hewletts Turnout where we bivouacked.

On May 25th about noon we went into camp on the west bank of Little River near Anderson's. At 3:00 P.M. I was ordered to take part of the battalion to Newell's Station near Jericho Ford, where a considerable force of the enemy had crossed, it seemed, without the knowledge of anyone, and to send Major Ward with six guns to a position on the right of Pegram's Battalion, wherever that might be. My orders were to report to the officer commanding the infantry sent to the same point, and to cooperate with him in arresting the advance of the enemy.

When I reached the place I found things in bad shape. Our infantry—Thomas' Brigade—had attacked the enemy, but were repulsed and were somewhat demoralized. I got five guns into position on the extreme left and awaited the attack I fully expected, but fortunately they did not advance. There was no general officer present and the subordinate officer seemed doubtful about staying there, as we were some distance from the main body of our army and he thought the force which he had failed to dislodge, were then aiming to cut us off.

As night came on the situation was uncomfortable as nothing could be heard from the hot fight going on nearly two miles to our right and there were no signs of the enemy in our front, although the infantry pickets several times reported them as advancing. On account of the dense woods nothing could be seen thirty yards away. The heavy firing on our right continued after dark, but finally subsided about 10:00 P.M. Left away off without information or orders, at 11:00 P.M. we withdrew and after a long slow march finally got back to Anderson's where we found the rest of the battalion but not under command of Major Ward; for he had been instantly killed in the severe engagement on that part of the field.

His death was mourned by all. To me he was uncommonly attractive. He was an unusually efficient officer, an intelligent and excellent Christian gentleman and a genial companion. I missed him sorely. I had just finished dressing his arm—pierced by a bullet in the Wilderness fight—when the order came separating us. In vain had I urged him to go to the hospital until the soreness of the wound should disappear—for at times it gave him pain. But no, he thought it a small matter and preferred to stay with the command. He was buried near where he fell before his men left the field, and the place marked, so that a short while afterwards, a young Richmond girl to whom he was engaged found his body and had it removed to Hollywood. Among the thousands of soldiers whose bodies rest in that historic spot there was no braver, nobler spirit than Major George Ward, of Mississippi.

After placing the five guns in position on Little River, May 25th, as previously mentioned, I sent Captain Wyatt to report to Colonel Cutts, acting chief of artillery, and by him Wyatt's battery was stationed two miles to my right and on the bank of the North Anna. On the 26th there was considerable infantry skirmishing and some firing by enemy artillery, but they drew no reply from us.

On May 27th the enemy were found to have disappeared from our front, and the battalion moved with Heth's Division towards Ashland. On the following day, the 28th, we marched by way of Atlee's Station to Mechanicsville and went into camp.

On May 29th, at 3:00 P.M., we followed Heth's Division two and one-half miles on the road to Hanover Court House and went into position after dark. We

remained in this position the 30th and 31st. In the forenoon of June 1st we moved with Heth to Hundley's
Corner and relieved the 1st Virginia Artillery after night-
fall. In all these five or six days no large bodies of the
enemy were to be seen, but daily skirmishing and
occasional artillery duels kept us on the lookout all the
time for what we all felt would be Grant's last desperate
effort to break through Lee's lines and make a rush for
our capital. To give some idea of the feeling in our army
and the spirit of Lee's troops, I append hereto the original
letter I wrote home at this juncture.[2]

On June 2nd at 3 P.M. we moved with Heth to the
extreme right of the enemy's line of battle, as we afterwards found. Just before day (June 3rd), at old Cold
Harbor, I received a message from General Heth to report
at once to him. Following his courier I found him near
Cooke's Brigade, the left of his line of battle, waiting for
me to go with him to select a position for my guns. We
found a suitable place about fifty yards to the left of
Cooke. Day was now breaking and the enemy's skirmishers, apparently within a hundred yards, opened fire
on Heth and myself. I suggested to him it would be very
hazardous to try to get guns into position at that point
after daylight, which would find them in full view of the
enemy, whose main line could not be far in rear of their
skirmishers. I proposed to seek and find a point nearby,
the approach to which would be less exposed. But he
insisted that that was the place and the only place for
artillery, it being essential for the guarding of the left
flank of our line of battle, there being no Confederate
force on his left, except some scattering cavalry. Under
an emphatic protest, I nevertheless had to obey his order.
I ought to have been notified in time to get my guns up to

_____

2This letter is reproduced in Appendix I.

Heth's line before daylight, as I learned afterwards other battalions had been put in position *under cover of darkness.*

As quickly as possible I brought up Wyatt and Richards under cover of some woods to within about one hundred yards, and then made a dash for the position designated by General Heth, instructing the captains to unhitch horses as soon as the point was reached and get them and the drivers out of range. The two batteries came into position in handsome style, and just as the guns were unlimbered the enemy's infantry opened on us, not a scattering fire of skirmishers, but with a perfect hail of bullets from their line of battle, just as I had feared. In less time than I can write it, both batteries were disabled. Not an officer escaped. Two were mortally struck and the rest more or less badly wounded. Only a few men were untouched. With these and my adjutant, Lieutenant Woodhouse, I managed to get two of Richards' guns run by hand to the right about fifty yards to a kind of embankment, an old fence line, occupied by Cooke's left regiment.

The line on which the guns were unlimbered was at right angles to Cooke's line, and his left regiment, where I placed the guns, was along the edge of a thicket, as shown by the diagram on the following page.

These two guns were used the entire day whenever the enemy attempted an advance through the thicket. Their lines could be seen from the right of Cooke's Brigade and I was kept informed of their movements. And a number of times during that terrible day a great voice on our right would call out, "They are getting ready! There they come! Give it to them!"

Feeble efforts at charging they must have been, for not a Yankee showed himself on our side of the thicket.

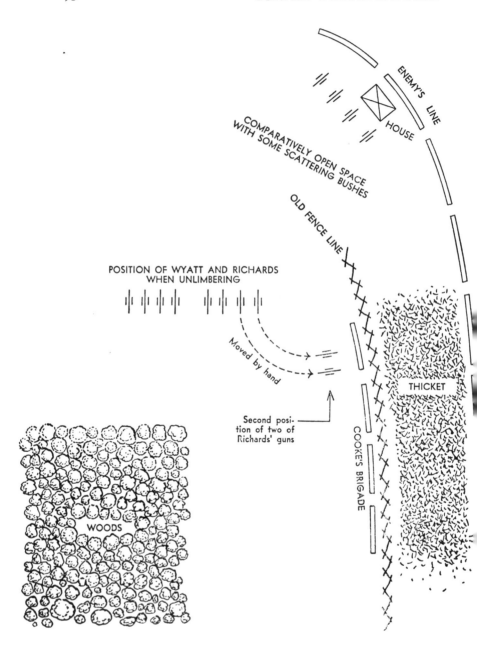

They kept up all day long a fusillade of small arms and shots from a battery on the extreme right. Neither Cooke's men nor our guns replied except when notified of their attempts at a charge. So incessant was their fire that all the trees and bushes along the little embankment behind which our men sheltered themselves were entirely denuded of leaves and twigs and the ground covered with clippings. Occasionally a man on our side would be struck. Three or four were wounded by balls glancing from our guns. I never anywhere saw such a needless expenditure of ammunition.

As well as I could judge, it was the purpose of our superior on that end of the line not to attack but only to defend. The enemy's line extended considerably beyond ours and an energetic commander would have attacked us on the flank. The fire that crippled my batteries was from our right front, as we unlimbered. I suppose Heth knew that their line overlapped his and hence his insisting on placing my guns at the end and at right angles with his line. It would have been all right if we had been posted there before daylight, but I was never able to learn who was chargeable with the failure to do so, as I never met General Heth again, and I can find nothing on record to clear up the matter.

The few men I had with the two guns behaved most admirably in every way. A member of the Mississippi Battery came to me about 9 o'clock and said he thought he saw Lieutenant Kearny, who had fallen under the first volley of the enemy, show signs of being still alive, and asked if he could not be brought in to our position where he would be less exposed. I told him if he was sure that he was alive, any two of his men who were willing to run the risk could fetch him in. Just then his arm was seen to move. At once two of them, Sergeant Dudley

and one whose name I do not recall, ran out and brought
him in, fixed his shattered leg as best they could and at
his request scooped out a shallow trench in the sand into
which they gently laid him. He expressed heartfelt grati-
tude to those men for risking their lives for him and
added: "Well, boys, if this is to be my grave, as probably
it will, I feel so much more comfortable here with you all
than out there in the rain," referring to the constant storm
of missiles sweeping over our abandoned guns. Kearny
got well and when I heard of him after the war he was
stumping around on a wooden leg.

As we went into position in the early morning I gave
my horse to my orderly with directions to gallop off into
the woods out of range. I saw no more of him. Not even
the ambulance men nor litter bearers could venture into
that belt of streaming minnies that poured all day long
over that devoted spot.

I myself received two severe contusions, one on the
point of my left shoulder so painful that I got one of the
men to see if possibly the missile had penetrated, but was
surprised as well as grateful to find it had not. A black
spot was left on my thick gray overcoat and my arm
turned almost black down to my wrist and was stiff and
sore for three weeks. The other was a staggering blow by
a piece of shell over my right lung causing hemorrhage.
Next morning pneumonia set in. But for this wound, I
would have had no thought of leaving the field.

I was sent to a hospital in the city of Richmond, but
finding it overcrowded I directed the driver to take me
to the American Hotel. Here I was fortunate in getting
a room, the attention of a physician and the kindly care
of Ned Alexander, a member of the Rockbridge Artillery.

PRIVATIONS AND PLEASURES OF THE
FINAL MONTHS

In a day or two my good friend, Alexander, put me on the train for Lynchburg with a furlough of 30 days in my pocket; and in another day I was at home. The next day I heard Hunter's guns at Lexington. It was curious to watch the effect of the cannonading on the servants. Instead of any manifestations of pleasure they all became at once serious and the older ones solemn. John Franklin, my army servant, was disposed to show off before the others, trying to appear totally indifferent to any supposed danger, but I noticed the same singular movement of his ears and an expression about his eyes that characterized him whenever a battle was opening. These manifestations all of our mess had come to observe and they afforded no little amusement to the other darkies about our headquarters.

We loaded two wagons with flour, bacon and other supplies and, in company with our younger negroes and some neighbors, we kept ahead of Hunter. A sort of council of war was held at Buchanan. Since it was the general opinion that Hunter was aiming for Lynchburg and would probably cross the mountains at Buchanan, we moved on to Big Lick (present day Roanoke). We then decided to cross the Roanoke River over into Franklin County where we went into camp at a Mr. Joplings. Here we remained until Hunter passed by in retreat to the western part of the state, pursued by Early.

Our stay at the Joplings was delightful to the few soldiers in our party—some four or five—and even the half dozen young ladies were not so unhappy as they were at the beginning of the refugeeing trip. The Joplings kept a most excellent table, being bountifully supplied with all the good things of the season. I remember with special pleasure the big family cherry pies.

By turns two men were sent every day across the mountain to Big Lick to reconnoitre and get the news. On the last day one of them, a young fellow named Morgan, was captured by Hunter's cavalry advance guard and carried off.

The day after I left home, father was informed by one of the old servants—probably Griffin Harvey—that some of Hunter's cavalry were in the neighborhood, and having heard that I was at home, would try to capture me. Their coming, with the purpose as reported, excited my mother, who was almost an invalid, and she at once burned all my letters written from the army.[1] This was something of a loss to me, as I had always written pretty fully about our campaigns and battles and expected to keep them for reference.

On the expiration of my leave, I reported for duty at Petersburg on the 6th of July (1864), and reassumed command of the battalion, which I found in position on

---

[1] Poague is referring to letters written during the first three years of the war.

the north side of the Appomattox River and three-fourths of a mile from Petersburg. During my absence Captain A. W. Utterback was in command of the battalion. Wyatt's and Richards' batteries, so badly damaged on the 3rd of June at 2nd Cold Harbor, had been overhauled and put in pretty good shape. The battalion, I learned, had been in no battle, but had been for some days engaged where I found it in a most disagreeable and trying sort of work—in line of battle though not entrenched, firing at the enemy and being fired on every day by all sorts and sizes of artillery and mortars. The experience with the latter was a new feature in the contest and one somewhat disconcerting at first. But our men soon got used to it. Two or three men were kept constantly on the watch, and as soon as the smoke of a mortar was seen, the warning "look out!" was given. Everybody watched the shell and those in and near its line of flight got out of the way or jumped into a little bomb-proof.

On the night of July 28th, the enemy's fire was very heavy. A big fragment of shell tore through the tent occupied by Captain Marmaduke Johnson and myself. At 10 P.M. I was ordered to the north side of the James along with a large force to meet an apparent advance on Richmond. This proved to be a diversion preparatory to springing a mine under the Confederate line before Petersburg, which was done early on the 29th,[2] with everything in their favor, yet Grant was badly defeated at the "Crater." On July 31st I was ordered to return to Petersburg, but was halted at the "Halfway House."

In a few days my guns were put in position opposite Dutch Gap, where it was reported the enemy had appeared in force for the purpose of cutting a canal.

---

[2]Poague erred by one day. The explosion of the mine and the Battle of the Crater took place on July 30, 1864.

Colonel Joe Mayo, commanding one of Pickett's regiments stationed at this place, soon satisfied himself of this and so reported to his superior, General Corse, I think. In a day or two General Lee, to whom Mayo's report had been forwarded, came over in person to see for himself. Owing to the thick growth on the river bank, nothing could be seen of the enemy in the Gap. Mayo was sent for and questioned very closely by General Lee as to the grounds on which he based his report. Mayo, who in person had reconnoitred the Gap every night from the bank of the river, gave his reasons, and among them was the fact that he could hear a windlass at work all through the night. General Lee with a twinkle in his eye said: "Colonel, did you ever hear of anybody digging a ditch with a windlass?"

"No, I don't believe I have, but those Yankees are using something of the kind and I don't know what else they can be doing," said Mayo.

For some time Mayo was twitted by his brother officers about his "ditch-digging windlass," but it was afterwards admitted that a chain running over iron pulleys was being used, but nobody could tell for what purpose.

Some years ago an article about Dutch Gap was published, in which the writer, an ex-Confederate, ridiculed General Pickett for reporting to General Lee that he believed the Yankees were tunnelling the Gap and that General Lee got angry at Pickett for reporting such nonsense, all of which is a myth. I never found out until I read in the report of Grant's engineer that the "windlass" was on board of a dredge scooping out an immense hole in the James to receive the debris when the bulkhead at the lower end of the canal should be blown out. The thing was a subject of much curiosity and discussion at the time among us Confederates. I hope Colonel Mayo, a most gallant officer, saw that report before he died.

My battalion was at Dutch Gap from August 24th, 1864, to the 2nd day of April, 1865. Up to the 1st of January, 1865, details from the battalion worked mortars, and sometimes guns, day and night—a period of over four months. All through the fall the men and officers suffered dreadfully from chills and fever. Sometimes it required nearly every well man for the details for three mortars.

Another source of suffering until cold weather were the mosquitoes. The men of the Mississippi Battery said they beat any they had ever encountered in the far South. As you walked along the river bank at night visiting the posts, officers could tell when they approached a sentinel by the sound of his mosquito brush. His hands were gloved or wrapped in a rag, and his head and face covered with the cape of the overcoat, the latter generally borrowed.

Aside from these serious drawbacks and in spite of them, our sojourn at Dutch Gap was more pleasant and comfortable than any previous seven months of army life. The location of our camp was the best possible, being in an extensive pine forest or thicket on a gentle southern slope of sandy soil, furnishing all the building material and fuel needed and a shelter from the winter winds. The men had comfortable huts and the horses also were under shelter. The light army rations were supplemented by fish and during the fall by some vegetables from two farms within our lines on the river. Not infrequently the men would chip in and buy a 150-pound sturgeon from fishermen; and sturgeon baked with black-eyed peas was considered a choice dish. General Pendleton on his inspecting tours nearly always dropped in at my quarters about dinner hour, knowing he stood a chance for a pretty good meal. No one enjoyed a good dinner more than he.

The men built a comfortable log church where services were held regularly by the chaplain, Reverend James M. Wharey, who was occasionally assisted in protracted meetings by visiting ministers. Among these was Reverend D. W. Shanks, afterwards of Lexington, Virginia. In this building all meetings were held for considering and discussing matters of general interest. After the Conference at Fort Monroe between Confederate leaders and Lincoln, a notable meeting was held and resolutions adopted reaffirming devotion to the common cause, and expressing confidence in our matchless commander. There was considerable display of oratory. In fact, one of the very best speeches I ever heard was that by a private in the Mississippi Company (Battery), J. Quitman Moore. I recall one old man, a substitute but a good soldier, getting up and saying he was willing to follow General Lee to the end, wherever that might be; that Lee was a great soldier and a good man and would tell his men when the time came to stop, for he was the only one that would know.

The amount of ammunition expended at Dutch Gap, if known, would be amazing. Even from our little mortars, the amount as reported from time to time by my ordnance officer, surprised me. From notes kept at the time I estimate the number of pounds of metal hurled into Dutch Gap as up in the hundreds of thousands. Ten times as much at least was hurled at us. In all these five months of incessant firing we suffered only two casualties, one killed and one wounded. This would seem almost incredible. Our men were protected by heavy parapets and strong bomb proofs. From what we could learn at the time and from their reports, the enemy suffered considerably as their working parties were necessarily exposed. One of their correspondents called the Gap "that hell-hole." Butler's working parties were made up of negroes, who were easily demoralized.

About the middle of October, Butler placed a lot of our men (prisoners) in the canal, not to work, but to stop our fire. I soon received an order from General Lee to double the fire and was directed by him through General E. P. Alexander to explain to my men the reason of this increase of firing. I was also directed to have a corral built around my mortars sufficient for 400 men and was told that when it was completed General Lee would send down from Richmond that number of Yankee prisoners to be confined therein under an adequate number of guards—this in retaliation. On the 22nd of October we were ordered to suspend work on the corral, inasmuch as Grant had taken our men out of the canal.

On October 29th an unusual phenomenon occurred as we sat at breakfast that bright clear morning. Smoke of shells bursting about Fort Harrison in plain view about three miles across the James was seen but not a sound heard. We were at a loss to know what it meant. Not a great while afterwards we learned of its being assaulted.

By mutual understanding there was no firing between our pickets along the river. Often I rode the whole length of the river bank to and below the Gap. About the middle of fall a piece of artillery—a 3-inch rifle—appeared one morning on the high bank below the Gap and sent an occasional shot at a team or a horseman away across the the bottom on our side. This was repeated several days undisturbed by our pickets on the bank across from it. I went down as usual to take a look at things and while dismounted and writing a note to the officer at the mor-

tars out near a swamp, the fellow spied me and forthwith
sent a shot pretty close to my horse which was grazing
around with the rein down on his neck. My frightened
horse galloped about the bottom for sometime before I
could catch him. As I rode leisurely back to my quarters,
an occasional shot was taken at me until I got out of
sight. I was naturally incensed by this sort of treatment.
So I had a well protected pit dug at night about 800 yards
opposite his position, and the next night got Captain
Williams to place his 3-inch rifle in it under Corporal
Gudger, a famous marksman with that weapon. He waited
for the Yankee to fire as usual at something and then lit
in on him, and in less than fifteen minutes knocked him
out completely, killing and wounding several of his men
and cutting down a wheel. The piece was soon deserted
and stood there all day and at night was taken away. It
never troubled us again.

Of course everything within sight turned loose on
Gudger, but he remained in his little bomb proof, snug
and safe, and after dark got back to camp. I had sent
word to our people at the Howlett house batteries and
other points of the coming duel, so that a large number
witnessed the fight and there was great cheering by our
people when the Yankees deserted their gun. Of course
they were at a great disadvantage in not being protected.
But he deserved what he got for having violated the
understanding we had been living under for two or three
months.

On the first day of January 1865 the bulkhead of the
upper end of the canal was blown out and thereafter not
much work was done. Occasionally we would send a few
mortars into the ditch. The canal was never used by the
enemy.

I can never forget the dinner I sat down to on Christmas day, 1864, along with the battery commanders of the battalion and a couple of officers from our ironclads. It was given by Private Dick Shirley, a noted *bon vivant* whose cook, George, was perhaps the best in the army. The menu consisted in part of oysters, fish, roast turkey, various vegetables, corn bread-a-la-Tuckahoe, and tropical fruits and the inevitable Christmas eggnog. Such an elaborate dinner was a surprise to us all and especially to the gentlemen from the navy. With appetites whetted by the eggnog, of course, nearly all ate too much and some of us paid dearly for over-indulgence. Two days afterwards Captain Penick, a pious Christian man and Baptist preacher, came to my quarters in a most penitent mood, bemoaning his imprudence and declaring that he had never before endured such bodily and mental suffering. It seems that Shirley had a friend in one of the blockade running ports whence he obtained many good things, and his cook was a great forager.

THE LAST CAMPAIGN

ON APRIL FIRST (1865), by order of General Long, I
sent Penick's and Johnson's batteries to report to Colonel
H. P. Jones at Petersburg. At 1:00 A.M. on the second
I received orders to report to General Pendleton at
Petersburg. Although I did not know the reason for these
orders, I felt something unusual was going on. At 9:00
A.M. I reported to General Pendleton with three batteries
and with him went out to the Turnbull house, the winter
headquarters of General Lee, where everybody seemed
busy packing up and removing the headquarters belongings. Just beyond the Turnbull house I found Penick
firing on bodies of the enemy on the left of the road which
seemed to run along the Appomattox. Johnson's battery
had been sent to a fort in rear of Fort Gregg. I was
directed by General Pendleton to take command of all
artillery that might be sent to that part of the lines.

Two guns under Major Brander, who a short time
before had been assigned to my battalion, were posted
about three-fourths of a mile up the road. Major Brander
used them with marked effect on the flank of the enemy

who seemed to be arranging his forces for a forward movement after breaking our lines and getting one or two forts. He threw back his left and sent forward a heavy line of skirmishers, causing Brander to move back to a second position from which he kept up a most disconcerting fire on the enemy's line. The enemy finally extended his line of battle across the road and towards the river.

I was informed by General Pendleton that Longstreet was on the way to Petersburg from the north side of the James and that it was extremely important to retard the enemy's advance until Longstreet could cross the Appomattox and interpose between the enemy and the city. General Pendleton said that the Turnbull house position should be held to the last moment, sacrificing the guns if necessary but saving the men and horses if possible. Guns were plentiful, men and horses scarce.

Utterback's guns had been sent upon their arrival to a position 500 yards to left of the road and somewhat in advance of the line of the Turnbull house. For hours Utterback's Battery in conjunction with some other guns —of what command I never knew—played on the gathering forces of the enemy until the Federal advance forced them back. I found Utterback and Johnson occupying a position about 500 yards in rear of the line of Turnbull's, from which they operated on the advancing enemy until withdrawn to the east bank of the creek and in the line held by Longstreet.

For holding the Turnbull house position I placed Richards' guns on the right and next to the river, then Williams' guns next and Penick on the right next to the road. On the left of the road were guns from other commands. The first assault on this part of our lines was broken and the enemy driven back into the woods along the road. After considerable delay another advance or

charge was made just as Longstreet's troops began
emerging into view from the end of the pontoon bridge.
We hoped to break up this advance also but failed because
of a force having been thrown on and in rear of our flank
under cover of the woods along the river, and thus we
were in imminent danger of being bagged. We managed
to get all our guns off safely except Richards' who, being
exposed to front and flank attack, had nearly all his horses
shot down. His men served the guns to the very last and
then escaped by putting the buildings between them and
their assailants, who halted as soon as they reached the
abandoned pieces.

I made my escape to the rear by jumping an ordinary
plank fence, fortunately being mounted on my brother
Jim's horse, Josh, who was a great jumper. I had gotten
but a short distance when a bullet whizzed near my head,
fired by an officer who was stopped by the fence. I turned
in my saddle and sent a shot in return and then waving
him an adieu, galloped to the road and joined our retiring
artillery which was safely withdrawn to the east bank of
a creek along which Longstreet's line was being formed.
Major Brander then took Penick's battery across the
upper pontoon, secured a position opposite the enemy's
left from which he stirred up great commotion in their
ranks about the Turnbull house.

The artillery rendered signal service that day by
enabling General Lee to get his headquarters safely
moved and by keeping Grant out of the city before the
arrival of Longstreet. Not an infantryman was on our
part of the line. I had a letter years ago from a Major
Nichols, adjutant of the brigade that charged and captured Richards' guns, wanting to know where the infantry
was that supported our artillery. He was surprised to learn
the facts. By the way, I think he must have been the

officer whose horse balked at the fence when he fired at a retreating Confederate mounted officer, whose horse made the fence which his refused. It is likely that I was the officer.

After Longstreet had established his line and the artillery was all posted—and while we were awaiting the expected advance of the enemy—I received a message to report to General Lee, whom I found at a small house nearby. He asked how many guns I had; also the amount of ammunition, the condition of horses, etc. I was then directed by him to move my battalion as soon as it was dark, cross on the pontoon bridge nearby and wait on the side of the road for Wilcox's division. I was to report to General Wilcox, who had been informed that I was to march with him, and follow his command. General Lee gave no intimation of our destination.

Several generals and some artillery commanders were in the little yard, having been summoned for the same purpose that I was, and from this fact it was surmised that the city would be evacuated that night. General Lee's appearance and manner were in no way different under the trying situation from what was habitual with him, except that his face was somewhat flushed. I and some other officers were amazed that he could personally give detailed instructions to so many officers. Under such unparalleled circumstances, directing the details of the evacuation and of the night march, dignified, serene, self-possessed, he appeared greater than ever before. I had seen him often in battle, had had interviews with him when he was under tremendous stress, but nothing before had so impressed me with his towering greatness.

As soon as it was dark enough to permit our moving without notice by the enemy, I withdrew the battalion, crossed the pontoon and waited for Wilcox. Just here our cook and our hostler found us, bringing a large pot of coffee kept hot somehow, along with plenty of rolls and an immense pan of fish caught on Saturday at Dutch Gap by a member of our mess, Lieutenant McCarthy, the acting adjutant of the battalion. We had tasted nothing for 24 hours and greatly enjoyed such an excellent meal.

Falling in behind Wilcox, we followed his division all night and the next day, the 3rd of April, towards Goode's Bridge, feeding our teams once, stopping a short while on the night of the 3rd and feeding horses and eating a scanty meal from the small stores of our commissary department. We reached Goode's Bridge the morning of the 4th and Amelia Court House at 1 P.M., where we remained till next day. The whole army seemed to be concentrating here.

I received orders from General Pendleton to equip my battalion thoroughly in guns, ammunition and horses from the numerous battalions of artillery assembled about the Court House. I was directed not to take any of McIntosh's equipment, since his battalion and mine had been selected to accompany the infantry then being organized into two corps, one under Longstreet, the other under Gordon. I was informed that this force of infantry and artillery was to be interposed between Grant's pursuing troops and our immense trains of artillery, ordnance, etc., which were to move on roads least exposed to the enemy.

The attempt to carry out this order raised a storm of protest among the battalions visited by Major Brander and my battery commanders. Major Brander ran into his own old battery where things were made pretty warm for him. A few guns with their ammunition were taken but no horses. The choice of these two battalions, I suppose, was due not to any superiority of men or officers, but to the condition of the teams which I learned were reported to be the best in the army.

On Wednesday, the 5th of April, I dined at Reverend D. W. Shanks' residence, where a most bountiful table was spread. Others also partook of their hospitality. While at dinner a report came that the enemy was advancing on the Court House and as some of our troops were placed in line near the Shanks' house and skirmishers thrown out, the inmates were much alarmed, but were somewhat reassured by our continuing at the table and finishing a hearty meal. My first and only interview with General Longstreet was on this day when I reported to him. He made a most pleasant impression, inviting me to a seat beside him and offering me ice water. His manner was very kind and polite.

Late in the evening of the 5th we resumed the march, following Longstreet's command. Our progress was slow and we seemed to be moving mostly on farm roads. Frequent halts were made. The men got some sleep but not the officers, who were strictly enjoined to be on the alert at all times and to see that the column was kept closed up.

Neither the battery commanders nor Brander and myself had had any sleep worth speaking of since the previous Friday night, until the night of Tuesday the 4th at Amelia. Here we did not get a chance to close our eyes till after midnight and then were roused before daylight. Passing through Deatonsville and crossing a stream called Bat Creek, we reached Rice's Station sometime on Thursday, April 6th, after a most tiresome march, threatened at many points by the enemy and detained while small bodies of cavalry raided the trains and burned a great many wagons. We were never out of sight of the smoke from those burning vehicles.

At Rice's the Federals began a serious attack on

Longstreet, who prepared to receive it with his whole force in line of battle. Upon this the enemy desisted and contented himself with skirmishing and random artillery shots, his purpose seeming to be to delay us. We were halted so often on this march that battery commanders were allowed to catch what sleep they could in these halts, Major Brander keeping watch at the rear of the column and I at the head. Orders were very strict against allowing any gaps.

About midday I was seized with an overpowering fit of drowsiness, so I proposed to Captain Penick, whose battery was in the lead, that at the next halt he keep watch while I would catch a short nap. To this, of course he readily assented. Impressing on him the strictness of the orders against allowing any intervals to occur, I dropped to the ground at the next halt and at once went to sleep. After a while I got awake; and looking up I saw no troops ahead of me and beheld Captain Penick with his back against a stump, sound asleep. On arousing him and starting the column, I told him I was obliged to place him under arrest. He admitted that I was right, but said that if he had believed that his life depended on it he could not possibly have kept awake.

After some minutes here came tearing back one of Longstreet's staff with orders to put the battalion commander under arrest for failure of duty. I protested against it, saying that the culpable officer was already under arrest. His reply was that he would not then place me in arrest but would report the facts to General Longstreet from whom I might expect to hear about the matter. But I never heard from him.

Captain Penick was greatly mortified, for he was a conscientious man. Just here I may say that loss of sleep, especially in this closing campaign, was the severest suffering by far that I endured in the whole war. It seemed as if we would never overtake the troops ahead of us and when we did suddenly come in sight of them, my heart dropped down from my throat and I felt a great burden lifted from me.

After dark on Thursday, April the 6th, the march was resumed and continued all night. We reached Farmville on Friday the 7th at 9 A.M. Here we got some bacon and corn meal and going on beyond the town towards Cumberland Church, I was directed to halt and cook rations. While this was going on an urgent order was received to hurry the battalion forward to Cumberland Church where the enemy was threatening our trains. Hastily the partly cooked food was seized by all hands, men and officers, and devoured as we marched. I had great difficulty in getting ahead, the road being blocked by wagons and vehicles of all sorts—the drivers panic-stricken and refusing to make room for us to pass. They thought the enemy was behind and that we were running away from them. Pandemonium reigned for a little while, drivers shouting and swearing and some abandoning their teams and taking to the woods.

Directing the leading battery to push through as fast as possible, I galloped around the jammed column and broke into it with drawn pistol, forced the drivers into a single column along the left side of the road and thus at last got a clear way on the right side for our guns. When I got them to understand that the Yankees were trying to get to the trains in front I had no further trouble. When we reached a blacksmith shop, for which point I learned the enemy appeared to be aiming, the head of the column was turned into a field on the right and as fast as possible the guns were thrown forward into line.

An advance was ordered and soon the position of

the enemy (infantry) was ascertained, and each battery taking the most eligible position to be had, opened on the enemy's lines which the pines and cedars pretty well concealed. The right battery, Williams', became separated in the advance and was caught by a body of the enemy slipping through the scrub pines and getting in its rear. The men barely escaped by running to the left.

Up to this time we had no infantry support and would soon have been forced back by the advance they were preparing to make. But fortunately at this juncture Mahone rapidly deployed his leading brigade and without halting an instant pushed it right through our guns and soon had the enemy on the run. Luckily Williams' guns and horses had not been taken off by the enemy and were soon recaptured. Williams and his men were soon at them and joined in the final repulse of the advance of Humphrey's Division. This performance of Mahone's men was as fine a piece of work as ever I saw. His skirmishers deployed at a run and moved forward like a lot of sportsmen flushing partridges and old hares among the broomsedge and scrub pines. The enemy made no further demonstrations at this point.

I looked up General Mahone and through him thanked the officers and men who so gallantly came to our aid at such a critical moment and recovered the captured battery. I found him sheltering himself under a poplar tree from a passing thunder shower and in a towering passion abusing and swearing at the Yankees, who he had just learned had that morning captured his headquarters wagon and his cow, saying it was a most serious loss, for he was not able, in the delicate condition of his health, to eat anything but tea and crackers and fresh milk. By the way, Mahone's troops seemed to me to be in the best shape of any of Lee's infantry and General Mahone was one of the very best of his subordinates.

Sometime in the afternoon the enemy attempted to break in upon the trains from the other side and nearly opposite our position. My batteries and a number of others were hurried across the pike and opened on a body of troops in the woods not more than 600 yards distant. Our cavalry attacked them in the rear and soon dispersed them, capturing and bringing into our lines General Gregg and a lot of his men.

At this point I met with General Pendleton, who told me of the interview he had just had with General Lee at the instance of a number of his generals and it accorded with the account published afterwards of that memorable interview. The enemy having been defeated in both of these attempts to cut in twain General Lee's column, did not molest us again. The developments of the enemy on both flanks, with what I learned from General Pendleton, made the situation for the first time look very serious to some of us subordinates of the artillery as we talked over matters that afternoon. But encouraged by what we had just heard of General Lee's views, we all took heart, feeling that whatever was possible to be done he would do and so gave ourselves no needless anxiety, but took great comfort in the thought of having such a leader to follow.

We moved on after dark on April 7th behind Longstreet's troops, but not long afterwards lost connection with him as we came up with the artillery and trains filling the road, his infantry passing on at the side of the road through woods and fields where we could not follow. So far as I could see or learn, I was at the rear of the army and hence felt much uneasiness, knowing that I should be utterly helpless if attacked by cavalry.

But my fears would be quieted by the reflection that our Commander was managing things.

About 10 o'clock we reached a point where the road was utterly impassable and the small field on the left was filled, it seemed, with hundreds of wagons and batteries struggling to extricate themselves from the miry soil. Being thus brought to a halt the men dropped wherever they could find a resting place and got a nap of about two hours. Fortunately, there was a good moonlight; and after the field was cleared of vehicles we managed to pick our way through, the teams being assisted through the worst places by the men. We came into what appeared to be a broad pike along a ridge at right angles to our previous course—where we found the going much better.

After marching a while through woods, horsemen were heard approaching our rear at a rapid gait. But before I could be informed they overtook the rear battery and much to the relief of the captain, settled the question of friends or foes by the party turning out to be General Robert Lee and a small escort. When the general reached me at the head of the column, he slackened his pace to a walk and asked how I was getting along. When I told him that one or two of the teams were much jaded, rendering our progress rather slow, he said: "If any of your teams give out, don't delay your command to try to get them along; perhaps you can reinforce them by horses from a caisson, which can be abandoned." Those were the last words addressed to me by the commanding general of the army. I had occasion to heed his instructions not long after he passed on.

About daylight on April 8th we reached comparatively dry ground and at sunrise came up with the rear of the army which had halted for a short rest and for feeding man and beast wherever any were fortunate to have food.

I soon got with Longstreet's people and kept with them all day on fairly good roads. Although moving all the time with an occasional halt, we had a day of quiet and refreshment for we seemed to have gotten to where the weary Confederate was at rest and the wicked ceased to trouble. During all the bright pleasant day not a gun was heard, nor smoke of burning trains seen. It was nothing like the awful three days preceding when cannonading, musketry, shoutings and yellings—tidings of disasters—greeted unwilling ears at almost every step and smoke of burnings hung like a pall over the path of our retreat. Indeed, it began to look as if at last we had gotten away from our pursuers. When at sunset we were ordered to bivouac for the night it seemed like old times. As the camp fires began to appear and our bands were heard playing at different points, we were again happy.

My orders were for reveille at 1 A.M. and at 2 o'clock to follow Longstreet on the road to Lynchburg. After a delightful sleep of four hours, our bugle sounded. A cup of coffee (real article), some corn bread and bacon made our mess a tolerable breakfast. Promptly at 2 A.M. on April 9th we pulled out into the road looking for Longstreet. Waiting a little while and hearing nothing of him, and thinking probably his corps had cut across the fields and were ahead of us, I pushed on and soon came up with a cannon unlimbered and pointed along the road toward Appomattox Court House. The sentinel could not tell me why the gun was posted there, nor could he give me any information about Longstreet.

I was a little puzzled as to what to do. If there had been any change in conditions affecting the march of my battalion I surely would have been notified, or ought to have been. Assuming there had been no failure in duty above me, and presuming that our cavalry was picketed to the front, I moved on. On reaching the village I came upon a cavalryman who informed me that General Rooney Lee occupied the place and learning where the General was quartered I reported to him for information about Longstreet.

"I know nothing of his whereabouts," he said. "Where are you going?"

I replied: "I had orders to move at 2 A.M. and follow Longstreet on the road to Lynchburg. I am hunting him."

He responded: "I don't think you'll find him ahead of you, but you will find the enemy not far beyond the village. Don't you think it would be well not to go any further, but wait until daylight and see how things look?"

This last sentence was accompanied with a smile and a slight twinkle of the eye as much as to say, "O, how innocent these artillerymen are." Of course I took the hint; dismounted the drivers and all hands went to sleep. It was just the beginning of dawn and shortly after sunrise I received a request from General Gordon to support him in a forward movement he was preparing to make. Accordingly I formed the battalion in line behind Gordon's left and on the left of the Lynchburg road. We moved forward in good style through a field, keeping a proper interval between the guns. Reaching the far side of the field we came on the enemy posted beyond an open valley at the edge of a thick pine forest. They had two guns near the Lynchburg road which opened on my right battery on the right of which I was riding along the road. It was not long before they were silenced and deserted. Probably some of Gordon's men had a hand in knocking them out.

Very soon a force of infantry or dismounted cavalry emerged from the pine forest, moving along the road as if to charge our position. This movement was soon checked. The other batteries had veered to the left somewhat and were halted at the edge of the open ground where it descended to the little valley and fired to the front shelling the pine woods. The left battery, with more favorable ground, got considerably farther to the front than the others. I myself stayed with the battery at the road expecting the way to be cleared soon, so that we could move forward by the road. It was not long, however, before it was learned that the enemy was in strong force in our front and I presume General Gordon found him to be far superior in numbers to his force and desisted from any further attempt to advance.

In the meantime, I got a pressing request from Captain Penick for a regiment of infantry to keep back a body of the enemy trying to capture him, until he could withdraw his guns. He was keeping them at bay with canister, which wouldn't last long. I sent him word that I would try and get him help and at once dispatched a messenger to General Gordon with Penick's request. The general replied that he would at once send the desired help. Soon another urgent appeal came from Penick who reported the enemy to be gradually closing in on him and stated that he would soon be out of canister. I myself then galloped to where I understood Gordon was and found him on the right of the road about 200 yards from the village sitting motionless on his horse with some staff officers and orderlies nearby and not a word spoken by anybody. Saluting the staff as I galloped past, I reined up at Gordon's side, saluted and asked where the regiment was that was to go to Penick's relief. His face was pale and I saw that he was laboring under some overpowering

emotion as pointing to his front, near where the left of
his line had rested before the advance, he said with
tremulous voice and heart broken tone, "That will stop
them!" and turned his face from me.

I looked and saw about three hundred yards away a
horseman at topmost speed with a white flag streaming
behind him and going directly towards the position of
Penick's battery. Not taking in the full meaning of the
thing and feeling somehow that General Gordon did not
care to say anything more, I turned to his staff and asked
what it meant.

"Surrender"! was the sententious reply. "Surrender
of what?" I asked. "Gordon's command or General Lee's
army"? "General Lee," was the only answer I got.

All at once my heart got to my throat and everything
around me became dim and obscure. As in a horrible
dream I rode slowly back to my right battery on the pike
trying to realize the full significance of what was going
on around me. Penick's guns were no longer roaring as a
short while before. A strange, all-pervading silence
brooded everywhere. As often as my mind reverts to that
particular hour, I am reminded of the expression in Rev-
elations, "There was silence in heaven for about the space
of half an hour," only substituting a very different word
for heaven.

Dazed, bewildered, without explanation, I ordered
the batteries to assemble at the road. As soon as the last
one, Captain Penick's, which sure enough that flying
horseman had saved from capture, joined the rear of the
column we moved slowly toward the Court House. Presently, I received orders to halt outside the village and
await instructions.

Soon officers and men pressed up to the head of the
column anxiously enquiring if it was true that General

Lee had surrendered. Nearly all crowded around Brander and myself as if unwilling to accept confirmation of the terrible news whispering along the column, except at the hands of those who commanded them.

Such scenes as followed were never before witnessed in the old Army of Northern Virginia. Men expressed in various ways the agonizing emotions that shook their souls and broke their hearts. Some cried like children. Others sat on the ground with faces buried in hands, quietly sobbing. Others embraced friends, their bodies trembling and shaking. Others, struck dumb and with blanched faces, seemed to strain their eyes to catch the form of some awful horror that suddenly loomed before them. But it is useless for me to try to picture the gloom and sorrow of that supreme moment. I have often wished some one could put on canvass the unparalleled scene in my battalion, with Gordon and his staff sitting on their drooping horses nearby—motionless, pale, speechless!

Soon the trying scene was ended by a dozen or more Yankees on foot running across the field to the battalion hunting the flag which by this time had been stripped from staff furled and securely hidden in the bosom of the color bearer. Not finding it, they came to me and asked that I order it to be delivered to them. This I declined to do—asking by whose authority they were on that errand. "Nobody's but our own," they replied, and as they became somewhat offensive in their remarks, I advised that it might be better for them to get back to their own lines.

A crowd of our men were gathering and listening to the colloquy and by their remarks, showing some feeling in the matter. My last remark was the signal for an outbreak of indignation, as they realized these fellows to be of the class of "flankers"—if not "bummers"—found in

nearly all armies. So our soldiers very emphatically
seconded my bit of advice, and bluntly informed them
that if they did not get away at once they would thrash
every man of them and began to shed their jackets and
roll up their sleeves for the job. The Yankees wisely
moved away toward their side of the field, muttering
threats, and saying we would hear from them again about
the flag. But nothing more was heard of them.

I then asked General Gordon what I must do with
my command. He said he had no orders for me, but that
I had better remain where I was, and that probably I
would soon receive orders on the subject. Before a great
while one of General Pendleton's staff came with instructions to withdraw the battalion to the north bank of the
stream near the village, park the guns and caissons, with
teams hitched and each company bivouacked near its
battery, make ourselves comfortable as possible and await
further orders.

Much has been said about who fired the last shot at
Appomattox. I don't believe anybody ever knew certainly
what command did, whether of the infantry, cavalry or
artillery. Many have claimed it as something to their
credit. I have never been able to see how anyone could
claim any special credit—or honor, as some have termed
it—for doing an act of duty after somebody else had done
a similar act, to repeat which would have been against
duty. The last shot on that field was determined simply
and solely by circumstances and not by courage and
fidelity to duty. To claim it as an honor implies a failure
of duty on the part of comrades. As a simple matter of
fact, I think Penick's Battery, of Halifax County, Virginia, probably fired the last cannon shot on our front.
It is possible that there may have been later cannonading
at the rear where Longstreet confronted the enemy. But

as the white flag which stopped our firing came from the direction of Longstreet's position, it is likely that his guns ceased before Gordon's.

After getting the batteries parked, Brander and myself pitched a little "A" tent not far from the creek on a bit of green sward, spread our blankets and at once dropped off into a profound slumber. Ah, the luxury of that long sleep still dwells in memory, and to think of it now is refreshing. The Yankee officers who called, some with cigars, others with something to drink, at once saw that it was useless to try to rouse us and did not tarry long. Doubtless they realized that men utterly broken down and stupefied from loss of rest and sleep, bewildered and crushed by the events of the hour and prostrated by the inevitable reaction of the occasion could not be expected to make very agreeable hosts. Except when occasionally interrupted and then only for a moment, we slept and slept during the remainder of the day and through the night.

Next morning I rode to General Pendleton's headquarters, learned the terms of the surrender and was much relieved to know that we were to be paroled and not to be sent North, as was feared by some. In going to General Pendleton's Headquarters, I passed a wagon, where a friend in the quartermaster's department called to me to come and get a blanket which might be of use to me in a Northern prison. I accepted the blanket—a new one and good—from a lot he was distributing, as we could hear nothing of our wagon which contained all our belongings.

Our headquarters wagon was never heard of until about a week after the surrender when one of our servants, Joe, who belonged to a Mississippian, came to our home—"Round View." From him I learned that our quartermaster, Captain Tulloss, took his train through Lynchburg to the neighborhood of Forest Depot, parked all his wagons, forges, etc., in a field, jumped on his horse and started across the country for his home in Fauquier County, Virginia, leaving no one in charge and making no effort as far as I could learn to communicate with me. After he thus abandoned his train, everything was soon plundered and taken possession of by the inhabitants of the neighborhood, both white and black. By this inexcusable course of the quartermaster, we at battalion headquarters lost everything, as did all the officers of every battery. Before leaving winter quarters I had provided myself with a new uniform including a pair of top boots, also a piece of English grey cloth which I was lucky enough to get from a friend through the blockade.

A number of relics and mementoes, consisting principally of official papers that had come into my possession with endorsements of distinguished officers, were stored in my "box" for safe keeping. I sent Joe back at once, on horseback, to see if he could find anything, especially of the papers; but not one thing was left. Horses, wagons, mules, forges, tools, and the contents of every wagon— all had disappeared. Tulloss lost his head, I suppose became panic-stricken and thought of nothing but his own safety. He was an excellent man and efficient in the management of his department under ordinary circumstances. But like most of the "bomb-proof" officials of the army, as they were termed, he was timid and easily demoralized.

Monday, April the 10th, was spent in fixing up the paroles of companies—officers and men and turning over the guns, ammunition and other equipment. Tuesday morning farewells and goodbyes were said, the battalion was formed in line, general orders read and the last command given: "The Battalion is disbanded!" The companies soon were out of sight. How long they kept together as companies I know not; probably they soon broke up into small squads.

I had thought of saying a few things to the battalion when last drawn up in the way of expressing my appreciation of their fine soldierly qualities ever since I had the honor to command them, especially in the recent trying days. But I found myself dumb—so utterly and unexpectedly overcome that I broke down at the very start—and was able only to utter in broken tones: "Men, Farewell!"

I speak truly when I say there has never been a day since, when I could dwell on that last scene without experiencing emotions of deepest grief and sorrow.

I must not forget to mention that our poor horses here for the first time suffered from hunger.

In the charge with Gordon Sunday morning, being on the main road on the right of the battalion, we passed a broken down wagon laden with corn in the ear. I hurried my orderly along the line to get as many bags from the drivers as he could find (many drivers always carried an empty sack for emergencies) obtain some help, and secure as much of the corn as possible. Thus we got a fair share of the much prized feed, for there was a general scramble for it by other batteries. What we grabbed up furnished a light feed for some of our horses Sunday evening, for although they no longer belonged to us, our drivers could not see them suffer without trying to relieve them. The enemy had no food for them. By Tuesday morning the horses had destroyed their collars for the straw they contained. Some men broke sassafras bushes and other shrubbery for them. Monday it was known that the people into whose hands they had fallen would not interfere with Confederates in taking such as they wanted; so that by Tuesday morning all the best animals had been appropriated. When I came to get one in place of the one the Confederate Government still owed me for (it having been killed in battle), the best I could get was an old fellow of not much value.

APPENDICES

APPENDIX I

Letter of Poague to his father, June 1, 1864, relating two incidents concerning General Lee

Line of Battle on Hanover C. H. road
10 miles from Richmond
June 1st, 1864

My Dear Father

I write home so frequently because I am sure you all are very anxious to hear from this army. The solicitude of the people distant from the army must be very great, because of the apparently unfavorable movements of our army in having at length reached a point so much nearer Richmond than at the beginning of the Campaign. On the other hand I doubt not the Yankees take great encouragement from the fact that their army is now within twelve miles of R———. But they could have reached the same point without firing a gun or losing a man. As it was however, they endeavored to run over Lee's army when placed across the path they had marked out, in the Wilderness and at Spottsylvania, and failing in this they did the only thing left them without going back, which was to "Sidle" around us. At the Junction Lee again confronted Grant but the latter repeated his old game rather than accept the wager of battle offered him. Again we have been in front of him for two days at this place, and it would not surprise me if he again shifts his position

without attacking—though he can't move much further
to his left before he reaches the James. Why did he not
attack us again at Spottsylvania? At Hanover Junction?
Why his delay now? If he had not been greatly worsted
at the Wilderness and at Spottsylvania we would not ask
these questions. After he patches up his Army and gets
reinforcements no doubt he will make another attempt
to get to R———. With the continuance of God's favor
this army will defeat him again.

Since beginning this letter heavy musketry and
cannonading has commenced on our right and is now
going on. Possibly Grant with the help of some of
Butler's troops is again trying the metal of the Rebel
troops. We at this time (8 A.M.) are on the extreme left
of our line of battle.

I will take this occasion to relate an incident or two
illustrating the feeling our soldiers have for Gen. Lee.
On the morning of 6th of May when the enemy had
gained some advantage over our troops on the plank road
in the Wilderness, and were pressing our men back when
Longstreet's troops came up and were hastily formed in
line of battle, and as their famous Texas Brigade started
forward passing right through my guns, Gen. Lee rode
along with it, having his head uncovered. This spectacle
brought our troops up to the highest pitch of enthusiasm,
but they did not forget that their beloved Gen. was thus
exposing his person greatly and the whole line called
out to him to go back! go back! and finally they told him
they would not fire a gun unless he went back. Entreated
thus by his troops and implored by members of his Staff
he was prevailed on to withdraw to a place not so much
exposed.

How the old General's heart must have swelled at

this display of filial regard and tender solicitude of his veteran soldiers under such circumstances.

Again at Spottsylvania Gen. Lee was at the position occupied by my Batin. (Battalion) when the Yankee batteries opened most furiously on the place as if conscious of the whereabouts of their great antagonist. A great big impulsive fellow, private Shirley of Utterback's battery, becoming uneasy for the safety of the Gen., politely but earnestly invited him to take a seat in the gun pit. The Gen. in his polite and pleasant way declined. Presently a shell struck very near and covered the Gen. with dirt. Shirley could stand it no longer, but springing forward, seized him (Gen. Lee) by both hands and implored and besought him to take a seat in the pit, and did actually drag Gen. Lee to a place where he was less exposed. These little incidents will serve to show how Gen. Lee's boys value him and love him. I would not have missed that spectacle on the plank road for a great deal. But here is an order to move—I still hope to hear from home some day. With best love for all I am

> your affect. Son
> W. T. Poague

APPENDIX II

War-time (1864-1865) Letters of Poague to his mother and brother

Near Dutch Gap
23 August 1864

My dear Mother,

Your letter of the 9th reached me last evening. This delay is one of the results of the quarrel now pending between the P.M. General and the President of the Va. Cent. R. R. about carrying the mails. From the great inconvenience and disappointment entailed on the public, this misunderstanding must involve matters of grave import. If it be a petty squabble about nothing, they both ought to be conscripted into the infantry.

I am relieved to know that John got home. I have a servant in his place. I think John had better stay at home till winter. Think it would be good for him to take a little exercise on the farm, at least enough to cure him of the "Spring Fever" which disease I fear had taken deep root in his system. He was not much to blame however, for life in the army is a very lazy one, and very few are proof against its effects.

Among these few I make bold to class myself simply because nearly all the time there is something for me to do which must be done. If I had only an occasional round of guard duty to do perhaps I would be as lazy a Rebel as could be found. I claim no credit therefore for my industry since I make a virtue out of necessity.

For the past week we have been trying to harass the Yankees and negroes who occupy Dutch Gap and are engaged in cutting a canal. Some times at night we open on them suddenly from a position just across the river from them and cause them to have very unsatisfactory naps.

We are now using some of our guns as mortars, and toss a shell every 10 or 15 minutes over into their ditch, keeping it up from morning till night. They are evidently very much annoyed by these shells judging from the commotion that may be sometimes seen among them from our look-out, and judging also from the number of guns they sometimes turn loose upon our "Swamp Angel." They have as yet done us no damage except smash a wheel.

In fact the Yankees at this point are not as bloody a foe as another we have to contend with, the musquitoes. I have heard many musquitoe yarns and storys but I believe they all fall short of the realities I have experienced in the past two weeks. I will not mention any particular performances of these insects lest you might think me guilty of romancing. No musquito yarn will ever be too absurd or extravagant for my credulity hereafter, and no tale of horrors with which musquitoes are connected will ever be beyond my belief nor fail to secure my sympathy.

An officer who is located near me here sends the worst cases he has for punishment to the picket lines in the swamp to fight and be fought by, not Yankees but musquitoes. They are not allowed to take their guns lest shooting at and being shot at by the Yankees might divert their minds from their agony. No wonder the inhabitants of the James River low ground look pale and sallow after having their veins depleted by these merciless blood-letters.

I'd rather take my chances in a country [swarming?] with lanncets that ancient terror of females, children and darkies—the old fashioned Doctors lanncet—[two words undecipherable] and living—than to have to spend my days in these swamps. The lanncet takes your blood, but leaves no sting behind, but the horror and agony of the smarting stinging and itching of these musquito bites for days after, is indescribable.

The only thing that makes them endurable by our soldiers is the thought that they are pepering the Yankees too. Indeed the people about here tell us the further you go down toward the Yankees the worse the musquitoes are. This may be true. If so I confess it is the only misfortune in which I have ever felt or could possibly feel for the villaneous scamps.

If it be the will of Providence that I shall pass through this war, and if it shall be my privilege as I hope it will to become an old man, and take my grandchildren on my knee and recount to them the trials suffering and horrors of the Great Revolution, perhaps no chapter in my narrative will so horror-up their little souls, and cause their flaxen locks to stand on end as the account of the doings of the musquitoes at Dutch Gap in the summer of 1864.

My health is and has been very good, and I never fail to have a good appetite for the vegetables we occasionally get. Watermelons of a respectable size can be had for five dollars.

When John gets well enough to travel on horseback please remember to send him down with Josh to exchange for Blanch. If my vest is finished send it also. I heard that Margaret Gray is with you. Give her my kindest regards.

I write home once a week, sometimes oftener. How often does a letter leave home for me? Give love to Pa and Frank and Miss [?] and believe your dutiful and affec't son.

W. T. Poague

Camp at Dutch Gap
5th October 1864

My Dear Mother,

I have been looking anxiously for a letter from home for some time. The failure to get any news from Rockbridge makes me think sometimes that perhaps the Yankees have been among you. I wrote to Pa sometime ago, as soon as I heard of Early's defeat at Winchester offering some suggestions as to what I thought would be best to do in the event of the enemy advancing towards Rockbridge. I hope there may be no occasion to adopt these suggestions. It seems that Sheridan does not venture further than Staunton at this time, but if reinforced he may yet attempt to reach Lynchburg. I feel sure however he will not get that far.

The newspapers have informed you I suppose of Grant's late freaks at his old game of "Bull in the pen." He got a little more of the Va. soil under his control, but we killed and captured a considerable number of Yankees, and the account balances largely in our favor. There is a considerable margin of soil yet remaining that we can afford to give up, and still keep Ulysses Grant out of Richmond. The lies manufactured out of his late operations will do however to gull northern people with for a while, but I think they will not last till the election, for which they are intended. With an ordinary share of the favor of Providence, I believe we will neutralize these influences brought to bear on the people by their falsehoods before the eventful 6th of November.

I think our prospects are unusually bright and hopeful. If the Lord of hosts will bless us in future as I believe He has done in the past, our independence is certain. Every day deepens the conviction in my mind that the God of battles has been with us and that our wonderful success (and it is truly wonderful when we consider all things) has been due to his direct interposition in our behalf.

I am still blessed with excellent health. The sick list in the Batt'n decreases very slowly. I fear the chills will hang on to some all winter. We are engaged as usual in hammering away at Dutch Gap. Have succeeded in pretty effectually breaking up their working operations. I am looking for them to make a dash across the river to capture our little mortars that have given them no rest for the past six weeks. Although they have used all sized artillery and mortars on us, yet they have never scratched a man. I believe the good Lord has shielded our heads in the hour of peril. On the other hand we have killed and wounded numbers of them. This we know from the lamentations and groanings that were often heard among them, and a few days ago I received a note from one of Gen. Lee's staff enclosing a piece cut from a Northern paper which acknowledged a considerable loss of life among them, and complimented our firing.

What is the news from Alice? I wrote her a letter some time since, but have heard nothing from them since. Give love to Pa and Frank and accept same for yourself. Remember me kindly to Miss Tirzah, and to all *patriotic* neighbors. I have no kind feelings to spare for any other sort.   Your affect. Son
                              W. T. Poague

Camp near Dutch Gap
26th Oct. 1864

My Dear Mother:

Your letter has reached me, announcing the illness of Father. I hope his sickness may be nothing more than ordinary chills & fever and that he may soon get rid of them. From the tone of your letter however I fear that it is something more serious, and I am very anxious to hear from home soon. Assure him of my most affectionate sympathy. I always remember him and you and brothers in my poor prayers.

I have not written to James for more than a month, first because I have had nothing in the world to write not having heard from home for nearly six weeks, and I could tell him nothing about myself here except that I have had the chills which would not interest him. Then too I have not been able to get any federal stamps. As soon as I come across any I will send you some. We are all busy preparing for Grant's expected attempt on our lines before the federal election. By the blessing of Heaven we mean to defeat him in all his efforts. Things in the valley don't turn out well for us some how. When I hear of these reverses I can but think of the time past when you used to follow "old Jack" (as he was *affectionately* called by us then) in his glorious races after the enemy as well as his skilful retreats. I cannot help contrasting the characters (*moral*) of the leader of the army of the valley in those days and of its present commander. I fear Gen Early doesn't pray as hard as Stonewall Jackson did to the Lord of Hosts who giveth victory to whom he will. Some might call this fanaticism. But still such thoughts (and many more) will pass through my mind in thinking over the news as we get it from the valley. I have great confidence in Gen Early's ability and admire

him for his high soldierly qualities, but would like him
still better if he were like Jackson in religion. I wish him
better success next time.

Do write to me soon Dear Mother and let me know
how Father is.

Give him my love and accept some for yourself and
Frank.

Your affec. Son
W. T. Poague

Near Dutch Gap
4th Nov. 1864

My Dear Mother,

Isabel's letter kindly written at your request, reached
me to-day (Monday.) I often wish I could have a letter
once a week from home however short it might be. You
can't conceive of the gratification it afforded me. Isabel's
letter was an unexpected pleasure, because heretofore
I always have to wait a great while for answers to my
notes, so that really I was not expecting it so soon
although extremely desirous to hear from you all.
Although the letter I recd today stated that Pa was
improving yet when it mentions the fact that the Doctor
was with him every night, I cannot help feeling quite
uneasy about him. I do trust he may continue to improve.
If he has been dangerously ill I am sorry that I did not
know of it, because I certainly would have made the
effort to go to see him. In very urgent cases only are leaves
of absence granted. In the course of a month there will
be no difficulty I suppose in getting off. I hope to spend
my Christmas at home with you all. I have had no chills
for some time, and feel better than I have done since they
got hold of me. I think now I shall be able to keep clear

of them. The health of the Batt'n is still improving and I trust this keen weather will give the finishing stroke to them.

The Yankee election and its future consequences is the subject of a good deal of talk and speculation here with us. Lincoln is believed to have been elected. Nearly everybody expected this, and are therefore not surprised nor disappointed. I had hoped for the election of McClellan because it could not have made matters worse, but would at least have been of some advantage to us in the exchange of prisoners and in ameliorating the barbarities and cruelties that have characterized its prosecution under Lincoln. I doubt whether McClellan's election would have shortened the war. The Northern people haven't got enough of the war yet. There is still too much hatred towards the South and pride and Fanaticism among them to stop at this stage of the contest. They still have a sort of hope that they can conquer us. Very well: let them go ahead.

They will have their eyes opened some day, and then they will be astonished at their present blindness. With the blessing of Providence in the four years to come as in the four that are past, we will maintain our independence. As for myself, although tired of this kind of life, yet I would not think of exchanging it for such a peace as Lincoln would offer. If I were to live three score and ten years, I would a thousand times choose to spend them as I have the past 3 or 4 of my life, than endure peaceful & quiet subjection to yankee rule.

Give love to Father and believe me your affectionate son

W. T. Poague

Camp opposite Dutch Gap
29th Decr, 1864

My Dear Mother,

Two more days and we will have done with the year
1864. I do not regret its departure. It has been to me a
year of more sorrow by far than any of my life. First on
the list of my griefs was that for the death of my intimate
friend Wilson Poague. Next came the sad tidings of the
death of my old classmate and friend Pendleton, followed
soon by that of Massie, another classmate and valued
friend. Then were snatched away by the relentless hand
of death my two young cousins Temple and Alice
Shields, then my friend Miss Abbie Chancellor and then
last of all came father's death, the source of a deep and
long enduring sorrow to us all. I am not lothe [*sic*] to
part with '64 because I hope that with it will pass away
the clouds that darken the horizon of our country, clouds
more threatening perhaps than any that have ever over-
shadowed us. I trust that '65 will appear as the dawning
of brighter days, and better times. I hope Mother you do
not allow yourself undue trouble about the unfavorable
aspect of affairs. I meet with some who are considerably
cast down. For myself while I cannot but regret our misfortunes in the field, yet I am not disheartened nor do I
suffer myself unduly to grieve over them. First they are
not beyond remedy, and even if they were, I feel that I
am not responsible for I think I have done all I could.
And if one does his duty he can leave the result with God,
feeling sure that for himself all things will be done well
and wisely.

Where is James? Have been looking for a letter
from him. Will write to him as soon as I learn his
whereabouts.

With the exception of our usual shelling of Dutch

Lee's Headquarters.

Junction of Plank Road and Willard's Furnace Road

LEE TO THE REAR

"The enemy had gained some advantage over our troops on the plank road in the Wilderness, and were pressing our men back when Longstreet's troops came up and were hastily formed in line of battle . . . as their famous Texas Brigade started forward passing right through my guns, General Lee rode along with it, having his head uncovered. This spectacle brought our troops up to the highest pitch of enthusiasm, but they did not forget that their beloved General was thus exposing his person greatly and the whole line called out to him to go back! Go back! and finally they told him they would not fire a gun unless he went back."

From Poague's letter to his father, June 1st, 1864

Line of Battle on Hanover C.H. Road
10 miles from Richmond
June 1st 1862

My Dear Father

I write home to acquaint you
because I am here you see are very anxious to
hear from this army the solicitude of the people
at Richmond from the army must be very great, because
of the apparently unfavorable movement [of] our army in
hearing at length the attacked point is much nearer
Richmond than at the beginning of the campaign —
for the others [means] I doubt not the Yankees
take great discouragement from the fact that
their army is now within twelve miles of
R— but they could have reached the
same point without firing a gun or

Facsimile of letter of Poague to his father, June 1, 1864, in which he refers to restraint of General Lee by soldiers when he tried to expose himself unduly in the Wilderness campaign. The original manuscript is in possession of Mrs. Henry G. Poague and is reproduced by her kind permission.

"They have used all sized artillery and mortars on us."

Gap each day, we have passed a quiet Christmas. The enemy have ceased entirely to reply to our fire, except with a few sharpshooters whose efforts thus far have been harmless. It will be some time I think before the enemy complete their canal.

Remember me kindly to Miss Tirzah and accept much love for yourself and little Frank. Hope James will be at home again soon.

Affectionately,
W. T. Poague

Camp near Dutch Gap
21st Jan. 1865

My dear Mother,

I have been expecting to see a notice of Father's death in the Gazette and perhaps the Central Presbyterian, but as yet none has come under my eye. It may be that it was in some number of the paper that failed to reach me. I had thought Mr. Junkin or some friend of Father probably would have had it done. Will you please let me know if such notice has appeared in any paper. If so can you send me a copy of the paper containing it. If not I shall send a brief notice to the Presbyterian. It will be simply one of fact and the time of his death.

Have you moved yet from the old house? If you have not been able to get any glass send me the number and sizes and if I succeed in getting a leave, I shall try to get it in Richmond and take it up with me.

I am glad to hear that little Frank has started to school and now that he is away from the crowd of little darkies with whom he used to run I think there is hope for him giving more attention to his book. Tell him I shall before a great while begin a book for the letters he promised me.

I propose to plant a garden this spring and I would like for you to tell me when and what to plant. Perhaps you could spare a few seeds to help me out for I think it will be rather difficult to find them about here.

I have been busy all week superintending the erection of a chapel, and did a respectable share of the work myself. It is nearly completed and will be a comfortable house when finished.

We have the promise of some of the big preachers in Richmond to visit us occasionally and I trust it may please the Lord to visit us too and grant his blessing on our labor without which all will be in vain.

Please let it not be long before I hear from you, dear Mother, for I sometimes get very lonely and feel like a single line from you would dissipate this feeling.

Your affectionate son
W. T. Poague

Camp Near Dutch Gap
28th Jan, 1865

My Dear Brother:

I am glad to see from the Lexington Gazette that the 1st Dragoons are in the county with the prospect of staying for some time. I shall direct my letter to Fancy Hill taking it for granted that you are at home. You can now dispense with the detail for which you applied, which, in view of the recent act of Congress (I believe it has passed both houses) will not be granted and if already granted is revoked by the act referred to.

I hope you will be able during your stay at home to get our business matters settled up or at least put in the way of being settled. It is very doubtful about my getting a short leave the 1st of March. Gen Lee requires now a statement on the application of the time when the officer was last absent, it being intended I suppose not to grant more than one leave in the winter. I shall nevertheless make the effort. Matters here are extremely quiet. At the beginning of the week we had a little excitement to break the monotony of the past month. Our fleet attempted to pass the obstructions (Yankee) with the view of going down the river and smashing up the enemy's shipping and using up the only monitor they have here at this time. Unfortunately the iron clads got aground just at the obstructions and were at the mercy of the Yankee land batteries mounting very heavy guns, the monitor and a number of gunboats for about 6 hours. Only one shot however penetrated disabling some $\frac{1}{2}$ doz men. I saw 15 inch shells strike the sloping sides of the Virginia and bound up a hundred feet in the air. One of our wooden boats that got aground was blown up by the second shot made at her, but none of the crew was lost having been transferred to one of the iron clads. The fleet finding that the obstructions could not be passed as they say, returned to Chafin's. I think they could have gone through the obstructions. But an old man commands the fleet and lacks dash and is entirely too prudent. He has officers under him who would have taken the iron clads in sight of Fortress Monroe. Every thing is frozen up even to the James which has a thin covering of ice. I have enjoyed myself skating the past two days. Do write to me soon. I get terribly homesick or lonesome or something. I hardly know what. I have had no letters from home since I left except yours.

    With love to all I am

                fraternally and affectionately yours

                    W. T. Poague

Dutch Gap 11th Feb. 1865

My Dear Mother,

Your kind letter of 31st ult. reached me some days ago, satisfying in some measure the incessant longing I have had to hear from home. This I hope is but the first of an unbroken succession of these welcome messengers from home. I never lose sight of the contingency that may some day deprive me of the means of communicating with home and while the privilege and opportunity exist I like to avail myself of them as often at least as it is convenient to write.

I am getting along in the usual way, enjoying excellent health and having a plenty to do. What with examining and endorsing official papers, visiting the trenches; inspecting the camps, visiting the hospitals, reading the papers and entertaining company I scarcely ever have an idle hour in the whole 24. In fact I have been so much confined at home that I am considerably behind hand in returning the visits of my neighbors and have laid off next week to square up on this score.

The week that is now closing has been an eventful one, and marks a new era in the army and I believe among the people too. Lincoln has very unceremoniously exploded the peace bubble, and most effectively stopped the mouths of reconstructionists and all others except the advocates of war. His proposals were insults added to injuries. The army is stirred up as one man, and spurn with indignation the infamous propositions of Lincoln. They accept war, protracted, never ending war, with all its evils and distress rather than yield themselves slaves to Yankeedom. As soon as the results of the peace mission were known my Batt'n passed unanimously resolutions indignantly rejecting the offered terms, renewing their vows of devotion to the great cause of Southern independence, etc. I think we have safely passed the greatest danger that has threatened us, that of a difference and division among ourselves, and with the blessing of Providence I believe we will gain our independence and secure a just peace.

Affectionately your son

W. T. Poague

Camp Near Dutch Gap
21st Feb 1865

My Dear Mother,

I wrote by yesterdays mail to James that my application for a leave was not approved, and intimated that I would drop a line again soon in regard to a few little business items. I have on hand the amount of the bacon account $486.00. If you and James (for I suppose you have qualified, or will at next court, [as] executrix) can get along in settling up without it, I would like to retain it for a while at least until I can draw pay of which nearly 4 months are due. When I shall be able to get it I can't tell for only officers on leave and soldiers on furlough are paid now. I shall go to Richmond in a few days and edeavor [*sic*] to have the accounts for wood settled, and will remit the amount by draft.

Ask James what he has concluded to do with Pelham. I think he will run considerable risk in leaving him at home. If he will contrive to get him to me I will take care of him. What do you think of the proposed enlistment of negroes. For my part I thought three months ago it ought to be done then. Everybody now in the army almost is in favor of it. If the bill should pass, probably one at least of our people would be taken. Horace or Jack or John. If the bill only called for volunteers I think they ought to be encouraged to enlist. I rather think however they will be put in by conscription. If John should not be willing to go into the army as a soldier and you should fear his leaving (as perhaps many will do) he had better be sent to me. I think he will be satisfied to stay with me.

In view of the uncertainty of affairs in our country, and the fact that the Yankees *may* occupy the valley some day and be your neighbors for a while, it would be well to attach the servants to you as far as practicable by kind treatment, and make them feel that it is their interest to stay with you. On this account I am glad you concluded to stay at the old place with them. I think our servants can be depended on with more confidence than the great majority of negroes, because they have always been well governed and well treated, and if they only knew the condition of the poor creatures who have gone to the yankees they would never leave you. But if the enemy were to occupy Rockbridge for any length of time it would be there as it has been everywhere else, most of the servants would leave under the persuasions and misrepresentations of the Yankees, and if that part of the valley should be devastated and laid waste then comes up that serious question (as it has often done of late to me) who will provide for and take care of you and little Frank. Well I won't know who may be the agent but I feel sure that God will not forsake you but that He will raise up some one to care for you. He is faithful and has He not promised to protect and provide for those who trust in Him even the widow and the fatherless.

O what a world of comfort and happiness in the thought, the belief, the conviction, the knowledge that God is unspeakably good to his helpless creatures, that He rules among men and among nations, that he will do that which is the very best for us and that to those that love Him all things shall turn out for good. It is in this way that I dispose of that question which under any other view of the case would be very troublesome and harassing. If you should have an opportunity to send me a box, one would come in very well in the course of a couple of weeks. Our stock of good things will soon be among the things that were. I expect to get this evening a bucket of oysters, the gift of a Rockbridge man who has always been very kind to me. Crigler, who used to live about Elliott's Hill sent me word to leave a bucket at my hospital on the pike where he will pass with his wagon and he would make me a present of a mess. He has frequently shown his kindness by acts of this kind.

We are to have preaching tonight by Mr. Shanks, formerly of Botetourt, a good preacher and a most excellent and agreeable gentleman. Tomorrow we propose to visit some acquaintances on the North side of the James where perhaps I may meet with Mr. Jenkins.

Ever keeping you all in mind with most affectionate remembrance,
> I am
>> Yours, etc.
>> W. T. Poague

> Near Dutch Gap
> 17th March, 1865

My Dear Mother,

If I have not been so prompt in writing as heretofore it is because of the supposed interruption of communication with the valley by Sheridan's raiders. But the reception of a letter from James postmarked 3 ult. reminds me that there is another mail route to the valley still open by way of Lynchburg, and I shall start this on that route

hoping that it may escape the Yankee brigands now
prowling about the base of the Blue Ridge, as rumour
has it somewhere between Ch'tv'll and James River. I say
Rumour, because I know nothing certain about them or
there [*sic*] whereabouts and I place no confidence whatever these times in the veracity of Madame R. The truth
is the impudent wench has lost standing in Lees army,
and I hope the time will soon come when we shall be rid
of her pernicious presence entirely. She had become so
audacious and persistent in circulating her falsehoods
that our old chief couldn't stand it any longer and gave
her a pretty strong hint to leave his army. In other words
an order has been issued warning officers against
circulating unfounded or unauthenticated reports and
directing all offenders in this respect (among officers) to
be court martialed.

I don't think my letters in the past have been remarkable for the amount of sensational news they contained
and in future perhaps you may have cause to grumble at
their barrenness in this respect. I have been so disgusted
and vexed by that class of long faced newsmongers and
sombre visaged rumour bearers that are constantly on the
lookout for news (especially, it would seem, of bad news
or at least it would be bad on leaving their mouths) and
for some one to whom they can tell it, that I have no
patience whatever with them and would almost as soon
meet a squad of Yankees as to fall into their company.
But it is gratifying to know that this class of creatures is
a very small and insignificant one in the army. I suppose
as long as the world stands there will always be some of
this class to afflict mankind both in peace and in war.
They are very much like another institution of the army
and scarcely less loathesome, I mean vermin. It seems
impossible for an army to get clear of either entirely.

The spirit of the great bulk of the army is most excellent
I think, if I may judge from the men of my own command, composed as it is of Mississippians, N. Carolinians
and Virginians. Though they may be naturally solicitous
as to the events of the not distant future yet they are
undismayed and if possible more determined than ever
to endure and fight through to a successful termination
of the war. As for myself I am not at all despondent nor
gloomy. Every time I sit down and think about matters,
and I make it a point every once in a while seriously to
reflect on the state of affairs and our future prospects, to
examine into the grounds of my belief, to contemplate
our cause in the light of justice and righteousness, and in
the light of God's usual method of destiny with nations
as revealed in the old Testament, in the light of his coun-
tenance and favor as most unquestionably manifested
toward us in the past four years, every time I think about
these things, the more my faith and hope in our ultimate
success are increased and confirmed. Think back of all
this, the immovable anchor of the soul amid the storms
and tempests of this world is the knowledge that God
rules, that He is a wise a just and a merciful Being, that
however the war may terminate, whatever may befall us,
He will overrule all so that that shall be done which will
be best for this people; and as individuals we know that
all things shall work together for good to them that love
Him. This, I declare to you my dear Mother, is the secret
of my cheerfulness, the ground of my composure in these
grand and awful days. The question with me is what is
my duty: It is not a difficult one to answer. My duty is
plain. It is to defend my country, and what does this word
country embrace in its meaning. It means the government
of my choice, the religion of my choice, the graves of my
fathers, property, friends, relatives, my mother and my

little brother. It means all that I love or value on earth. Yes this is my duty, and as far as in me lies I shall endeavor to perform it; and when ones tries to do his duty there is little room for despondency or unhappiness.

James letter was an unexpected pleasure to me. I was glad to learn that he had succeeded in putting our affairs in a shape to be settled up soon. He asks in this last letter if I attended to the little item of business with M. Blair & Co. I think I mentioned in two of my letters that it had been settled. This makes me think some of my letters have not reached home. I have written every week and sometimes oftener. I presume I shall have the pleasure of seeing him before long here with the army. I saw Mr. Jenkin last week, spent a delightful day with him and Mr. Shanks at Henry White's quarters. Mr. J. is preaching in the Texas Brigade. Mr. Shanks preached several times for us and with good effect I think. Our chaplain Mr. Wharey is on a leave now in the valley. He expected to spend his time about Brownsburg. I invited him to call and see you if he could, and recommended that he should call on my pretty cousin Rebecca, as I thought it was time for him, a preacher, to be looking out for a wife. If he has not been gobbled up by the Yankees I suppose he would return via Lynchburg and in that event would be sure to stop and see you. Please do remember me to Cousin R and say to her that I did not recommend her to my friend W. nor do I recommend him to her. I never meddle in such matters, too prudent for that. But tell her I heard a gentleman of intelligence and taste pay her a mighty splendid compliment in the presence of Mr. W. and I am almost sure he has strolled up to Falling Spring neighborhood and if so I can very well account for his overstaying his time as he has done. If my conjectures are correct, tell her I shall certainly haul him up and possibly a court martial will be the result, unless she intervenes for him.

Now Mother, write often if able, and if not able, I will not expect it.

With a heart full of love for you

I remain yours etc.

W. T. Poague

APPENDIX III

Letters Received by Poague, during the Reconstruction period, from Confederate comrades.

Monk's Corner Octob. 19th 1865

My Dear Col.

If I mistake not I promised to let you hear from me. I am rather slow in fulfilling that promise, I admit; but it has not been that I have forgotten you. I shall ever be grateful that a kind Providence threw us together, hope that our friendship will only be cemented by time, that it may be profitable to us both. Nor can I forget the fact that I already owe much to your kindness. This summer has given me an unwonted time for thought, for self examination, & for review of my course during the last few dreadful years. And I confess it with shame, there is little to comfort myself in these reflections. I can perceive little or no progress in an intellectual point of view or in that infinitely more important matter *piety*. I believe it is undoubtedly true, from my own experience, that war is terribly demoralizing to a nation. I trust that my life in the army was not altogether thrown away. There are some scenes to which I can look back with pleasure & no feelings of self-condemnation. But I fear that I will never attain to that degree of piety which I might have attained but for misspent time there. I shudder to think that I was not only making no progress but actually going backward in the Christian life. But for a merciful God where would have been the end?

I need not trouble you with an account of all my travels after I left you. I wandered about for several weeks seeking rest & finding none. But have finally pitched my tent, & expect to winter here at any rate. I am in Wythe County 9 miles East of the County town (where I formerly preached). I have charge of 3 churches. One in half a mile of me the other some 9 miles off in opposite directions. I preach at each once in three weeks, and also expect to preach in the afternoons somewhere in the neighborhood. The congregations are quite small, not more than 100 in all three combined. Religion is at a low ebb in this region. The members of the Church are not as consistent (some of them) as they ought to be; and they form a small body compared with the mass of the people. There is a great deal of practical & some real infidelity especially among the men. Have nothing to do with religion, never attend church etc. There is little hope of accomplishing anything with those who have grown up to middle life in the midst of these influences. There is much hope of the young.

Every thing is quiet in a Political view. The election just over, little interest in it. All felt the importance of electing such men to Congress as could take the oath. Among this class there was little choice. Much trouble experienced from the negroes. But there are comparatively few in S. W. Va. and I think this country will recover from all material effects of the war in a very few years. And, by the way Col. it is the finest country in the world, not excepting your lovely valley. Mark my prediction it is going to take the lead of all the rest of Va. I have seen with pleasure your advertisement of a school. I hope you may be eminently successful & useful. Have you heard

any thing from our army friends? Dr. Nash particularly.
I am anxious to hear whether he got off safely. I saw
one of Capt. Penick's men in Wytheville a few weeks
ago. I don't know whether you recollect him. His name
was Mote & had been very recently transferred to W's
Battery. He could give me no information of any one else.
And so old Gen. Lee is one of your neighbours. If [*sic*]
am almost inclined to wish I had my college life to go
over again that I might be one of the old gentleman's
boys. What does he teach? I did expect to be a somewhat
frequent visitor to Rockbridge. You can imagine why,
but all my hopes in that quarter are *smashed*. So my only
hope of hearing from you is by letter. Write to me & let
me know all about yourself. And if you ever have occasion
to travel this Va. & Tenn. R. R. be sure to stop & pay me
a visit. I am staying at the house of Sam. R. Crockett
(related to old Col. Davy) near *Max Meadows Depot*
which is my P. O. Though we have no regular mails yet
letters thrown on their own responsibility some how or
other & in some time or other generally reach their
destination. I hope this may be the case with this one.

Your sincere friend
J. M. Wharey

Vernon, Madison Co., Miss.
Oct 30th 1865

Col. W. T. Poague
   Fancy Hill,
     Va.

My Dear Col.

    I can impose upon myself but few tasks which are
more congenial than that of writing to one for whom I
have, ever since our first meeting, felt the warmest friend-

ship and in whose success both as a soldier & civilian I have felt the greatest solicitude. Times have changed very materially since we seperated [*sic*] at the ever memorable [Appomattox] Court House. I can scarcely realize the situation, & sometimes hear the roar of artillery and rattle of musketry in my sleep, and occasionally lie in my bed waiting for the hateful Revilee [*sic*]. I preserve my equilibrium generally pretty well until some emancipated Black begins to cut figures, or some straggling Blue B-lly boasts of cutting our feathers, then I want to be in old Virginia at my same old trade. Col. you know you used to fight us *mighty* hard. I have heard it whispered in camp, that you wanted to get the starch out of our shirts. I think you succeeded particularly on the last campaign. But notwithstanding your *fondness* for ordering the Madison Arty to the front, there was not a man in the whole company who did not respect you as a Patriot & gentleman. But I am diverging, too much, considering my sheet, to answer all the kind inquiries made at the suggestion of Joe. I was delighted to hear from Joe & so of the whole household. The news of his safety spread like electricity from house to Quarters. In all Africa there was never such rejoicing. I am glad Joe still holds on to his rebel proclivaties [*sic*]. He will be a grand exception when he returns. Tell him all are very anxious to see him both white & black & all hope to see him the same good old nigger Joe. His Sister Delia, is at home. None of the Negroes have left since he was at home but Hugh & Milly. On the upper plantation none have left. His Sister Delia says he must make haste & come home for she wants to see him mighty bad. She has a little boy that she calls Jim, after her brother. Tell Joe I have not heard from Jim. Tell Joe when he comes home that if he will go to Richmond and get my baggage from Mrs. Lipscomb

& Mr. Viles I will refund him the money for his expenses home, when he gets here. Excuse this short note. This is the only piece of paper I can muster about the house. If at any time you find a leisure moment none would better appreciate a line from you than your friend & wellwisher

Joe T. Lipscomb

PS   Should you ever visit Miss. dont fail to come to see us. The family have heard us speak so often of you that they feel as if you were an old acquaintance.

Newington, Feb 14th 66

Dear Col

Doubtless you will be surprised to know that I am still in Va. Unforeseen events have prevented my departure for Texas & I have been compelled to defer my trip till next fall. Your verry kind letter was received shortly after its date. I was pleased to hear that you had given D. Tyler a good recommendation for really I think he justly deserved it, he is a noble little fellow & was ever at the post of duty in times of need. I understand that his Father (Col. T.) has succeeded in recovering his property in Washington that had been libeled during the war it is verry valuable & will be particularly acceptable at this time his family being in indigent circumstances. I returned from Washington a few days since haveing spent a week there with my southern friends verry pleasantly. I am so thoroughly disgusted with this Jacobine congress that I did not deign to enter its halls, the galleries are crowded with a conglomeration of yankees and negroes who applaud, huzza & shout whenever anyting [*sic*] is said with reference to the latter which you know is the principal theme. The more I see of the yankee character the more I dispise & abhor them, how totally different from the southern gentlemen in all their actions. they have as a general thing no politeness, no generosity no feelings of delicasy. I have seen ladies enter the street cars and be compelled to stand while the yankee soldiers & citizens remained seated perfectly unconcerned.

I am in hopes Col that you have so arranged your business affairs as not to be kept so constantly engaged. How do you like school teaching? And what is the prospect now of that matrimonial alliance which you spoke of forming "when the war was over"? As I anticipate remaining in the "Old Dominion" for some time at least I again extend to you a most cordial invitation to visit me as soon as you conveniently may. I want you to see some of our fair ladies and when you do you will doubtless confess that old Va (*i.e.* east Va.) is really hard to beat. I am still pursuing the study of law and must acknowledge that I am better pleased each day having time to digest many points which proved unintelligible while hurrying thro the course at the U.V. I have been enjoying myself considerably during the winter, been attending some parties & sleighing, have two fine horses & a good sleigh.

The farmers in this vicinity are generally engaged fencing their fields & preparing for corn & the wheat is looking badly.

Col it always affords me great pleasure to hear from you. I must therefore request that you favor me with more frequent communications, with the hope that my expectations will be realized I remain ever your

sincere Friend, Mc

N. B.   Direct to Aldie, Loudoun Co.

Waverly Walker Co. Texas
February 17th 1866

My Dear Friend:

As Houston starts in the morning for Va. I will write
you a few lines to be carried by him. He and I came out
here soon after Lee's surrender; *i.e.* we started, and
reached here shortly after Kirby Smith's. We didn't hear
of the surrender of the latter until we had got as far as
west Ala.—dodging the Yankees, who were swarming
through that state and Ga. But we were then in no mood
to turn back. I at first thought of going on to Mexico,
but a little sober reflection brought me to the conclusion
that it would be wise to remain in Texas long enough, at
least, to make a little money before venturing into a for-
eign country. H. and I have both been teaching and, considering everything, have done very well, particularly H.
I am teaching now at Waverly where H. has been heretofore. It is a good community, the best I have found in
Texas and I have peregrinated considerably over the
mammoth state. I think Texas very much over-rated. Her
present prosperity is more apparent than real, the result
of her isolated condition during the war, her exemption
from its ravages, and, comparatively, from its inconven-
iences and burdens. There is an immense amount of very
poor land in the state, yet there is undoubtedly a great
deal of rich land, *in spots.*

I rec'd this evening a letter from Cousin Lizzie Brown
in which she informed me where you were and what
doing. "Tempora mutantur, etc." Since I have recovered
from severe billious fevers I had, by way of accli-
mati[zati]on, I have enjoyed excellent health. You probably heard when I got out of prison. I had started down
to the army to see whether I had been exchanged, and if
not, to get my parole-furlough renewed, when I heard of

the surrender. At that time it was impossible to get any reliable news in the valley without being subjected to a world of painful rumours for a week previous. As soon as I became convinced of the dreadful truth, I determined to strike for Johnston's lines, which I did, via Salem, Christiansburg, Floyd, and Carroll Cos to N. C. There I fell in with H. and—to be brief, here we are in Texas. It is my fixed purpose to go to Brazil, but for certain reasons have to postpone it for a year or two.

Sincerely your friend,

W. Morton Brown

Canton, Mi. July 26th, 1866.

Col Wm T. Poague
  Lexington Va.
    My dear Sir:

It was, I assure you, with feelings of very deep gratification that, I received, not many days since, a pleasing evidence of your kind remembrance. Accept, I beg you, Sir, my grateful acknowledgements, and if it should anything avail, receive, along with them, the assurances of the high, and unaffected admiration, which I entertain for yourself, as a patriot, a Christian and a gentleman. I shall ever bear with me, a proud recollection of my fortunate, and privileged soldier-association with one so pure, so true, so gallant and self-sacrificing; and the only regret that will accompany me, will be the consciousness of having myself accomplished so little for our great cause, compared with those rich offerings, which were cast by my honored commander on the common altar.

Our condition, as a people, is a very sad, and I might almost add, a hopeless, one, at least, for many years to come. But, so firm, and abiding is my individual faith

in the eternal and indestructable character of those great
ideas of Right, Truth and Justice, that lie at the founda-
tion of the social order, that, I cannot yield the conviction,
that, they will ultimately triumph, lift up our fallen cause,
and vindicate our heroic dead. I believe it, and shall
bequeath the belief as a proud, and patriotic legacy to my
children. It may not happen in our day; but, sooner, or
later, to this complexion it must come, at last. When I
remember the heroism, the devotion, the lofty self-
abnegation and immortal valor of those glorious heroes,
who, for long years, marched to victory and death, under
that proud banner, that now lies, folded, in monumental
glory, I cannot, without first renouncing my belief in the
Just and divine economy of the universe, believe that they
have labored, suffered and died, in vain. On the contrary,
indications are even now visable [*sic*] on the political
horoscope, of great, and important changes in the fortunes of the country, looking to a final overthrow of the
genius of revolution, that has, so long, devoured the land.
The Radical party (though still, numerically, powerful)
is beginning to tremble, and is looking, fearfully, out for
the coming of "Birnam wood, to Dunsinane." It feels
and fears, that, *it has gone too far,* and is nervously appre-
hensive that it will meet a terrible rebuke at the approaching, fall elections. I think there will be large Democratic
gains, in a *few* of the Republican States; but, I can see no
reason to encourage the hope, that, a coalition between
the Northern Conservatives and the United South, can
effect anything against the consolidated power of the
Radicals. I have, for this reason, opposed the sending of
Southern delegates to the Convention at Philadelphia,
believing that we had performed our whole duty in sending representatives to *Congress.* The Federal Parliament
(cant we call it, Barebones?) is the proper, and constitu-

tional power, before which to make tender of our desire
for reconciliation, to the offended Government; and if it
has seen fit to spurn the manly offer, it were unbecoming
of our manhood to crave as a gracious, and inestimable
boon that august privilege, for which, in our heart of
hearts, we have no sort of reverence or regard.

Pardon me, Sir, for indulging in this dreaming,
"Lotus-Eating," while coasting along the shores of the
high and holy memories, which your honored name
evokes, in my mind, and heart, from the shadowy past;
and ascribe it to the influence of that ardent patriot hope,
which, even in this moment of darkness, fails not to
occupy the chiefest place in the thoughts and affections
of a people who are joined together in the solemn
communion of sorrow.

Adieu, Sir! I shall always remember you with kindness, mingled with a sentiment of pride in the feeling
and assurance that your name will live, in character of
light, in the annals of the Southern Race!

With great respect, Sir,

Your Obedient Servant

J. Quitman Moore

[Editor's note: Poague wrote across the envelope which
contained this letter: "From 'Quit' Moore, an extraordi-
nary man & a capital soldier of my Batt'n. Was with me
as orderly detailed from Ward's Miss. Battery. W. T. P."]

Jackson Mississippi.
Nov: 27th 1867.

Dear Sir:

The last intimation I had of you was through my
friend Dancy who is now a student at Washington College. In July '66 I had the pleasure of receiving a letter

from you in reply to one which I had written informing
you of your election to an honorary membership in a
literary society at Madison College. I have often thought
of you since the memorable adieu at Appomattox, and
have as often wished that I could be and talk with you
face to face. Often time's have my thoughts reverted to
the scenes of by-gone days' so frought with pleasurable
recollections, and Ah! what a pleasure 'twould be to
behold the familiar faces of my old comrades once more.
But alas! I fear 'twill never be my good fortune to realize
that pleasure! for whilst some are still permitted to enjoy
the blessings of life, others must have been hurried to the
dark and silent tomb. I feel sad as I think of the time when
we were once united in a common cause, full of hope,
and high in spirit, battling for God and our native land
—for all our exertions were in vain, and the noble efforts
of our gallant dead to maintain the glory, the integrity
and independence of the once proud and sunny South,
like the brightness of a summer's day, was but momentary.

As early as June '65 we were told in a proclamation
by the President that the war was virtually at an end, and
that peace, that sweet winged messenger of love, was
extant the whole country o'er: but if this be peace, then
God deliver us from such a thing throughout all ages
to come! Here in our very midst, where nought but perfect
submission to the will of the conqueror has existed since
the cessation of hostilities, the freedom of the press, one
of the first and greatest guarantees of the American Constitution, has been denied us—and by whom?—Brevet
Major General Ord, an insignificant military satrap
clothed in a little brief authority, with all the arrogance
of a Napoleon, has defied the very laws of the government
under whose authority he is now acting. On or about the
4th of this month Major W. H. McCardle of Vicksburg,

published in his paper, The Vicksburg Daily Times, certain comments upon the errors and usurpations of Gen Ord, and also advised the people, through the columns of the same sheet, that if they voted at all to vote against a convention. For this act McCardle was arrested and imprisoned by order of His Satanic Majesty King Ord 1st. Finding his dungeon anything but a pleasant abode he accordingly applied for a writ of *habeas corpus,* which was granted, and the trial came off before His Honor Judge Hill in the U. S. Circuit Court at this place. Burwell conducted the suit, assisted by Major Swayne, a judge advocate to the U. S. Army, who delivered a sort of explanatory speech. Ex-Governor Sharkey, our Senator-elect to Congress assisted by Mr. Marshall and the Hon. Walker Brook of Vicksburg appeared on the defense. The case was disposed of yesterday in a very unsatisfactory manner, and as the matter now stands, McCardle has given bail to the extent of one thousand dollars for his appearance before the Supreme Court of the U. S. next month. I shall endeavor to send you a copy of the proceedings in this case very soon, as it seems to have created a great deal of interest in this section of the country; that is if you desire it.

Pardon me for dilating as I have, and excuse the liberty which I take in thus addressing you, but believe me, Sir, when I inform you of the high estimation in which you are held by myself and the residue of the surviving numbers of the "Madison Artillery." Your name will never be forgotten by the Mississippians who formed a portion of your command in the recent struggle for liberty and independence, and your face is as familiar and your appearance on the battle field of Appomattox when I felt for the last time the hearty grasp of your hand as fresh to my memory as if it were but yesterday. In con-

clusion allow me, Sir, to ask of you, the favor of sending
me at your earliest convenience a photograph of yourself,
taken if possible in the old Confederate uniform; for
next to our friends' faces is their pictures. Hoping that
I may hear from you soon, I remain very truly and

Respectfully Your Friend

A. H. Ware

P. S.   Could you let me know whether Lieut. T. T. Hill
is dead or alive? And Major Brander's address also.
Col. Wm. T. Poague
Fancy Hill Rockbridge Co, Virginia

Warrenton March 2 1869

My Dear Colonel
    I received your letter some time since and would have
replied ere this But my business for the last month has
kept me vibrating between this place and Balto Md so
constantly that I have hardly had time to eat in fact I have
not taken time to eat a respectable meal for the last month.
    I can assure you that I was more than glad to hear
from you—often since the gloomy day of our separation
at Appomattox CH. (Devil take the place. Im not recon-
structed yet) I have thought of you, and like yourself have
almost determined to write you a letter, but let the subject
drop, "for no good reason I'm sure." I though[t] that
perhaps it was incumbent upon you to open the subject
rather than myself. Be this as it may, Im truly glad to hear
from you. In reply to your inquiry as to what I had been
at since the surrender, I will answer that upon my arrival
home I found myself without means of any sort. I sold my
army horse for one Hundred Dolls, bought some clothing
for myself & family (which has increased since the war)
Then went to work in my old business, County merchant

Nov 1st 1865. from May until this time I was actg as fire insurance Agent for a Balto Co.

When I came home I found myself hopelessly (almost) in debt without any means to go into business of any kind. Until I was getting to be in (Sept 65) a fit subject for the lunatic asylum, when a kind friend loaned me Eighteen Hundred Dolls and on the first Nov, I started a small dry goods store (dont keep whiskey) at my old stand in this place. In 1866 I made six thousand clear & I made "two" last year. I came out about square. I have reduced my old debt from eighteen thousand dolls to about seven and now have a pretty good prospect of getting out clear in about two more years—if Providence will assist me and I keep my health.

On my return from the Army, I made a solemn promise & covenant in remembrance of Gods protecting care during the war that I would devote myself for the remainder of my life to his service and to the payment of my debts. I think I begin to realize that he has helped me to surmount some of my difficulties and blessed my labors in his cause. I found when I came home my church scattered, the edifice almost ruined, and no one disposed to make it his or her business to better things. After a great deal of hard work we have gotten our church handsomely frescoed. Our membership has been doubled since 1865, and we are now paying our pastor one thousand dolls. per annum.

Notwithstanding the loss of time and other things during the war, I think I have gained materially in hard experience & judgment and perhaps after all, I have only *gained* not lost any thing.'

Im sorry to hear of your ill health. May be that is a warning to you to be a "Precher of righteousness" rather than lawyer, schoolteacher or tiller of soil. Think of this.

You were a good soldier for Jeff. Why not stake as you did for the lost cause your all in the service of Jesus. Address Lieut Brown & Weems Balto Md. Capt. Tullos[?] at this place, Fry at Waynesboro (Genl Early is acquainted with the place) McCarty, Oxford Mississippi. Mc is married, and has a *Babie*. You see he is preparing for the next war. I have no photograph of myself that I could send you at present. I will be in Balto in a few days and I will have myself *struck off* & send you one on my return home or rather will exchange with you.

If you ever come over this way I hope you will come & see me. If you will take my fare I promise your board & lodging shall cost you nothing. If I could get you here to see some of the prettiest sweetest Presbyterian girls you ever saw, you would underscore that *would like to be married* with emphasis and be very strongly and strangely tempted to carry the desire into practical effect. By the way Col., real genuine love has a most excellent effect on old Bachellors, and I think I can truthfully say that a man (generally speaking) isnt much acct till he is married, a good man well yoked together, is allways a better man by being married, but a bad worthless fellow isn't any acct anywhere, the woman gets the worst of it in such a case. Excuse this rambling letter. I have just written down almost without thinking whatever popped in my head.

Truly your friend

A. W. Utterback

T. T. Hill, Culpeper CH
Shall be always glad to hear from you etc.

The STATE

TERMS:

The only Evening Daily	Daily	$3.50
Daily Circulation (5000)	Weekly	1.00

Richmond, Va., 17 May 1877

Col. W. T. Poague
Buffalo Forge
My dear Sir

I am greatly obliged by your kind favour of the 8th inst. The paper goes to you regularly.

It is praise indeed to be praised, as a soldier by one who so distinguished himself, every body knows, as the commander of Poague's Battery & Poague's Battalion.

Yours very truly,
Jno. Hampden Chamberlayne

APPENDIX IV

Lee's approval of Poague's request for mortars and post-war letter of Lee, presumably to Poague.

Hd Qrs. Batt'n, 24th Aug, '64

Maj.

A slow fire was kept up on Dutch Gap yesterday from a Napoleon. The enemy as usual replied with vigour. The officer in charge of the gun reports that the enemy used a Napoleon, 3 inch rifle, a 20 lb Parrot and a small mortar on him. No casualties. The damage to the parapet was repaired last night and the work strengthened, but not in time to get a gun in this morning: there will therefore be no firing today. What is the prospect, Major, for getting some mortars?

Very Resp'y
Your obdt. Serv.
W. T. Poague
Lt. Col. Art'y

to Maj. C. Pickett
A A Gen

* * * * *

Hd Qrs Chesterfield
Aug 24th

Reply forwarded calling attention to Col Poague's request for some mortars. Much annoyance can be given the enemy should we obtain them. This has been recommended for some time back.

Does the idea meet with the Genl's approval. Respty request a reply.

G. E. Pickett
Gen Com.

* * * * *

Hd Qrs: 26 Aug '64

Recd & referred to Col Baldwin with the request that he procure some mortars for Col. Poague. Two Coehorns.

R. E. Lee
Genl

* * * * *

Ordnance Office A.N.V.
Aug. 26th 1864

Reply returned. Two Coehorn mortars and four hundred pounds of ammunition forwarded for Col Poague today

Briscoe G. Baldwin
Lt. Col Ord. A. N. V.

* * * * *

Head Qts A. N. V.
26th August 64

Res. referred to Colo Poague for his information

By order of Gen Lee

W. H. Taylor

739   AAG

* * * * *

Letter of R. E. Lee, presumably to William T. Poague.
The letter was found in the Poague papers.

Lexington Va. Dec 11th, 1869

Dear Sir:

The enclosed letter has been rec'd from a committee
of thoroughly responsible gentlemen in New Orleans. It
explains and commends itself. I have consented to act
a chairman of the local committee in this county; and as
such shall be gratified if you will co-operate with me on
the committee. It is not expected that individuals can
subscribe largely; but it is hoped that the aggregate from
this county may be a valuable addition to the fund, if the
committee act with diligence. The character of the gentlemen composing the committee in New Orleans is
believed to be sufficient guarantee of the proper
distribution of the funds collected.

Any sum collected can be deposited with Mr. Friggat,
Cashr of the Bank of Lex.

Very Respectfully

R. E. Lee

EDITOR'S ACKNOWLEDGEMENTS

I am indebted to Colonel William Couper of Virginia Military Institute, who originally made the typescript for me of the Poague Reminiscences, examined certain records at the Court House, supplied some of my explanatory notes about local places and reminded me of many incidents about Colonel Poague as an officer during our Cadet days.

Robert Selph Henry personally searched the records in the National Archives and confirmed Colonel Poague's own statements about his military record.

B. E. Powell, Librarian at Duke University, opened all the files of pictures and photographs, gave me unlimited time and made my visit to the Duke campus most enjoyable.

Colonel Murray F. Edwards of Virginia Military Institute, a classmate of mine, furnished the photograph (made in 1913) of Colonel Poague on his horse leading a parade in Lexington in front of the Cadet Battery, Matthew, Mark, Luke and John, which Poague had commanded a full 50 years before.

I also received assistance from Francis P. Gaines, President of Washington and Lee University; Rev. J. J. Murray, Pastor of the First Presbyterian Church in Lexington; Robert W. Jeffrey, Public Relations Officer at Virginia Military Institute; E. Griffith Dodson, Clerk of the Virginia House of Delegates; E. G. Swem, retired

Librarian at William and Mary College; Edward E. Barthell, Jr., of Ludington, Michigan.

All of these gentlemen contributed to the accuracy of this book by wholeheartedly digging back into their dusty files to answer my questions or to furnish requested documentary evidence.

Seale Johnson's many warm and heartening letters during my assembling of this material extended far beyond his professional interest as the publisher and added to my own enthusiasm.

Bell Wiley's discerning introduction reflects his careful study of the manuscript and his keen interest in it.

M. F. C.

INDEX

177